REVISION

GUIDE TO RAPID REVISION

CANADIAN EDITION

Daniel D. Pearlman
University of Rhode Island

Paula R. Pearlman

Lawrence G. Hopperton
Seneca College

Prentice Hall Allyn and Bacon Canada
Scarborough, Ontario

Canadian Cataloguing in Publication Data

Pearlman, Daniel D.
    Guide to rapid revision

Canadian ed.
ISBN 0-205-26821-8

1. English language — Errors of usage.   2. English language — Rhetoric
3. Editing.   I. Pearlman, Paula R.   II. Hopperton, Lawrence, 1957-   .
III. Title.

PE1460.P42   1997   808'.042   C96-932028-0

 © 1997 Prentice-Hall Canada Inc., Scarborough, Ontario
A Division of Simon & Schuster/A Viacom Company

Allyn and Bacon, Inc., Needham Heights, Massachusetts
Prentice-Hall, Inc., Upper Saddle River, New Jersey
Prentice-Hall International (UK) Limited, London
Prentice-Hall of Australia, Pty. Limited, Sydney
Prentice-Hall Hispanoamericana, S.A., Mexico City
Prentice-Hall of India Private Limited, New Delhi
Prentice-Hall of Japan, Inc., Tokyo
Simon & Schuster Asia Private Limited, Singapore
Editora Prentice-Hall do Brasil, Ltda., Rio de Janeiro

ISBN 0-205-26821-8

Vice-President, Editorial Director: Laura Pearson
Acquisitions Editor: Rebecca Bersagel
Developmental Editor: Lisa Berland
Production Editor: Marjan Farahbaksh
Copy Editor: Vivien Young
Editorial Assistant: Shoshana Goldberg
Production Coordinator: Jane Schell
Cover Design: Petra Phillips
Page Layout: B. J. Weckerle

Original English Language edition published by Allyn and Bacon, Inc., Needham
Heights, Massachusetts. Copyright © 1997.

1 2 3 4 5 W 01 00 99 98 97

Printed and bound in Canada.

Visit the Prentice Hall Canada Web site! Send us your comments, browse our
catalogues, and more. **www.phcanada.com** Or reach us through e-mail at
phabinfo_pubcanada@prenhall.com

CONTENTS

Arranged alphabetically by
Correction Symbols

CONTENTS

*Instructor's
Symbols*

CONTENTS

PREFACE

Too often, writing skills are considered important only in English composition classes. But effective writing is a skill that applies across the curriculum. Frequently, students receive higher marks because they have expressed themselves clearly and logically, and have eliminated the need for "guess work" on the part of the instructor. This is true not only in the English class, but also in business, applied arts, and technology subjects. Furthermore, businesses that will employ students after graduation recognize the need for clarity in written communication. The Conference Board of Canada, a professional consulting group made up of the largest employers in this country, issued a report entitled *Employability Skills Profile* in which it discussed the requirements of the work-force of the future. Two of the essential skills it specifies are the ability to read, comprehend, and use written material, and the ability to write effectively. Clearly, effective writing has both short- and long-term benefits for everybody.

Rapid Revision, Canadian Edition, continues the thirty year tradition of its U.S. counterpart by helping to address this need. Unlike traditional English handbooks that provide extensive discussions about grammatical constructions, developmental writing, and rhetorical modes, *Rapid Revision* focuses only on the revision process. It is intended not only for composition classes, but also for technical and business writing, ESL, creative writing, and virtually every subject that requires writing. It is intended to act as an "instructor-over-the-shoulder," providing local and specific direction exactly where and when it is needed. The emphasis is on brevity, accessibility, and practicality.

A Review of the Major Features

1. *Instant access to information:* An outstanding feature of the *Guide* has always been the alphabetical arrangement of its contents in accord with the correction symbols in common use throughout the country.

Massive cross-referencing reveals the network of logical relationships among the "info-bites" that appear under separate headings. Other major aids to information retrieval are an exhaustive *Index* at the back of the book and the list of *Topical Contents* in the front that facilitates classroom study of whole topics like "Writing Style" and "Sentence Correctness."

2. *Compactness:* Even the longest sections, such as "Commas" or "Variety in Sentence Patterns," take up only a few *pages* as compared to long *chapters* in the usual college English handbook. For the student, such brevity means an effective job of revision in a minimal amount of time.

3. *Focus on problem solving:* There is not a word here that does not contribute directly to revision! Rules and principles of grammar and rhetoric are stripped down to a functional minimum. In the belief that a well-chosen example speaks louder than pages of abstract explanation, the pedagogical emphasis is on the illuminating example, and whatever explanations are necessary are linked to concrete examples modeling the solution of specific problems.

4. *Clarity:* The style throughout is direct and to the point, neither patronizing nor condescending. The author assumes that the reader is an intelligent seeker of guidance through the brambles of written usage.

Features New to the Sixth Edition

1. Completely new are the sections on "Word Processing" and "Idiom." The section on "Idiom" takes a further step, since the last edition, toward making this *Guide* more useful than ever to ESL instructors.

2. Many sections have been revised for this edition. Those featuring the most significant additions are **Agreement**, with its discussion of Collective Nouns; **Article**, with an explanation of Countable and Uncountable Nouns; and **Tense**, which now includes advice on using the present tense for plot summaries and presentations of an author's ideas. *"Words Often Misused: A Glossary"*—under **Wrong Word**—has also been

expanded. The result of the many changes that have been made should be a *Guide* that is even "friendlier" than before to traditional and non-traditional students alike.

3. The list of correction symbols has again been enlarged to include some new ones that instructors should find useful (such as several different symbols for the different types of problems encountered under **Logic**).

Daniel D. Pearlman
Lawrence G. Hopperton

TO THE INSTRUCTOR

I have long felt that the process of revision, central in the development of writing skills, has not been given the full attention it merits among books published for courses in English composition. Most composition handbooks follow a sequential and topical plan designed for *study* of the problems of writing but not necessarily for their immediate solution. Students who turn to these texts for help when revising papers that the instructor has marginally annotated find that they lose time hunting for the passages relevant to their particular problem. In fact, they must often read as much as a full chapter for each error they have made.

The present *Guide*, planned entirely with the realities of revision in mind, gives students *immediate* answers to specific problems, offers sufficient information to solve them, and yet does so with *brevity*. Using the book independently, students may feel as if an instructor were personally going over their papers with them point by point in conference.

Among the major time-saving features of this *Guide* are its compactness and the alphabetical arrangement of its contents. Another convenience is a table of correction symbols that doubles as a table of contents. The table presents the most common symbols used by English instructors throughout the country, and on the inside back cover there is space for students to list extra symbols that you may use from time to time. In the text are many realistic examples, often culled from actual student papers, of various types of writing deficiency. Many of these examples are followed by brief explanations that show exactly how to apply the general rule for revision.

Because the *Guide* is designed for independent use by students, you could have your classes spend a period now and then revising their papers, *Guide* in hand, under your direct supervision. The clear, compact treatment of each topic in this *Guide* should enable students to overcome a number of their weaknesses in short order; meanwhile, demands on you for individual help will be reduced to a workable minimum.

Guide to Rapid Revision is valuable both in courses where a traditional handbook of composition is assigned and in those, also, where no such handbook is used. The *Guide* substitutes for the larger handbooks because it contains an adequate treatment, despite its small physical compass, of the basics of English style, usage, and mechanics.

A topically organized listing of all sections of the *Guide* is provided on the next page to facilitate your using it as a classroom teaching text. For example, instructors interested in focusing for part of the semester on topics such as sentence correctness or punctuation will find listed under each topic the relevant sections in the *Guide*. It is hoped that instructors will be pleasantly surprised to note the considerable attention paid in so brief a guide to many matters involving writing style, and not only matters of basic correctness.

TOPICAL CONTENTS

Instructors who would benefit from a handbook-style *topical* approach to the concepts covered in this guide will find helpful the following logical groupings (with some inevitable overlap) of related sections:

TO THE STUDENT

This book is designed to save you many hours in revising your compositions. Its explanations of English usage are brief, clear, and to the point, and it includes realistic examples that you can use to correct your specific shortcomings. Years of teaching experience have convinced me that most of your writing problems can be eliminated in short order. In keeping the book short, I have tried to include all information that could cast real light on your writing difficulties. Each time you revise, you learn the principles of English usage so that you do not repeat the same mistakes.

HOW TO USE THIS GUIDE

If your instructor uses correction symbols and you are not certain of their meaning, the alphabetically arranged table of correction symbols found at the beginning of this book will tell you what the symbols mean and what page to turn to for help. This book avoids lengthy grammatical analyses of your writing problems. Specific examples—combined with short, concrete explanations—show you how to overcome your weak points. Extensive cross-referencing, such as the advice in the "Paragraph" section to "see **Coherence** and **Transitions**," enables you to find further information related to some special aspect of the problem at hand. Pursue such cross-references if you have time. Assume, however, that the *essential* information you need is already provided in the section you are reading.

Special spelling problems are handled in the sections on abbreviations and numbers and in the *"Words Often Misused: A Glossary"* section at the back of the book. Otherwise, for the usual misspelled word, refer to your dictionary. (Computer spellchecks are fine, but they are still not as reliable as a good dictionary.)

You will find this *Guide* a valuable reference for your formal writing and revision needs. *Formal* writing is more conservative in grammar and phrasing than *informal* writing. The emphasis in formal writing is on the objective, impersonal communication of ideas and information, whereas informal writing tends to focus on self-expression—the communication of feelings—and highlights the writer's own personality. Almost all the writing you will be asked to do in school or in the business and professional world is of the formal sort.

GUIDE TO RAPID REVISION

ABBREVIATIONS ─────────── ab

Spell out words in full and do not use telegraphic prose.

As a general rule, do not use abbreviations in formal writing. Some common abbreviations to avoid in your writing are *&*, *gov't.*, *B.C.*, *U.S.A.*, *thru*. Use *and, government, British Columbia, United States of America, through*.

NOTE: *U.S.* may be used as an adjective *(U.S. foreign policy)*, but neither *U.S.* nor *U.S.A.* should be used in formal writing as a noun *(made in the U.S.)*.

Especially avoid using *etc.*, short for *et cetera*, meaning *and so forth*, or *i.e.*, meaning *that is*. If you really want to say *and so forth*, or *that is*, write it out. With *et cetera*, it is usually better to write out the specific ideas you have in mind rather than to ask your readers to guess at what you mean.

EXCEPTIONS: With proper names, abbreviated titles are preferred: *Dr., Mr., Messrs., Ms., Mrs., Jr., Sr., St.* (Saint). The names of academic degrees or professional designations are also usually abbreviated: *B.Sc.* (Bachelor of Science), *M.A.* (Master of Arts), *C.G.A.* (Certified General Accountant), *P. Eng.* (Professional Engineer).

A second exception to remember is in the use of French abbreviations for surname titles. Only the abbreviation for Monsieur takes a period, *M.* Madame, *Mme*, and Mademoiselle, *Mlle*, do not take periods.

Standard abbreviations such as A.M., P.M. (or a.m., p.m.), A.D., B.C.E. and those of certain well-known commodities, organizations, and government agencies such as *TV, VCR, CAA, RCMP,* or *NATO*, are also acceptable. When citing a less well-known organization, give the full name of the organization at first mention; then use its abbreviation thereafter, preferably using periods: Canadian Automobile Workers, *C.A.W.*

NOTE: Most abbreviations are capitalized. When in doubt, refer to a good college-level dictionary.

ABSTRACT
abst —————————— # EXPRESSIONS

1. **Add a word or phrase to the abstract term to make it more specific.**
2. **Replace the abstract term with a word or explanatory passage that is more specific. (See *Vagueness*.)**

1. ABSTRACT TERMS

Abstract words and phrases, like *beauty*, *evil*, and *progress*, have meanings that are somewhat different for each reader. Perhaps you are certain of what you mean by *progress* in a statement such as this: "Canada has made great progress in the last fifty years." But your reader may not know what you mean until you use a more *specific* expression such as *technological progress* or *economic progress*.

To avoid vagueness, you would no doubt need to explain an expression like *economic progress* even further. Do you mean that a greater percentage of the population is employed? Do you mean that people have more disposable income?

The effect of explaining yourself further is to get more and more *specific* and *concrete* in presenting your ideas. The more precisely you define your ideas, the less you risk being misunderstood.

2. CONCRETE TERMS

A *concrete* word refers to an actual object whose nature is generally known. For example, we all know what *tree* stands for. However, when the tree you are writing about plays an important role in your composition, it is better to use an even more specific concrete expression, like *elm* or *oak*. It is like zooming in for a close-up in a movie:

ABSTRACT: Politics unfairly determined the results of the recent election. [Many of us, in attempting to explain the problems of society, take the lazy way out by shrugging our shoulders and blaming everything on politics.]
REVISION: A last-minute public smear campaign together with private blackmail unfairly determined the results of the recent election. [It turns out that the abstract *politics* was screening some rather interesting concrete realities.]

ABSTRACT: The success of computers has been due to the acceptance of technology. [This is vague and oversimplified. Does the writer have some specific ideas in mind that have led to the acceptance of computers as the following revision indicates?]
REVISION: The success of the home microcomputer has been based upon the simplicity of software and the low price of equipment.

ADJECTIVE ———————— adj

1. **Change the marked word to an adjective.**
2. **Change the marked adjective to the proper form.**
   (See *Comparison*.)

I. PREDICATE ADJECTIVES

An adjective modifies, or describes, a noun or pronoun. Usually, an adjective occurs right next to the word it modifies: the *delicious* coffee. But sometimes the adjective is separated from the word it modifies by a verb, called a linking verb: The coffee smells *delicious*. The adjective *delicious* modifies the noun *coffee*. Adjectives that come after a linking verb are called *predicate adjectives*.

One common writing error that students make is placing an adverb—instead of an adjective—after a linking verb: The coffee smells *deliciously*. The most common linking verbs are all forms of *to be*, such as *is, are, was,* and the following verbs of the five senses: *sound, smell, look, feel, taste.* Use an adjective after these verbs.

WRONG: My roommate felt *badly* about his recent grades.
RIGHT: My roommate felt *bad* about his recent grades.

Feel (Look) Good Versus Feel (Look) Well

Ordinarily, *well* is an adverb. Use *well* as an adjective — after *feel, look,* and so on — only when you mean the opposite of ill. It is no compliment to tell a friend that he looks *well* today unless he has just recovered from an illness. If you simply mean that you admire his clothing or haircut, tell him that he looks *good*.

WRONG: More muscle definition would look *well* on her.
RIGHT: More muscle definition would look *good* on her.

2. CORRECT FORMS OF ADJECTIVES

Adjectives can be used to indicate degree as well as comparison. The three forms of adjectives are the regular, comparative, and superlative. (See also **Adverbs**.)

1. *Regular Adjectives:* Use the regular form of adjectives when you are not making any comparison.

   He is *big*.
   She is *smart*.

2. *Comparative Degree:* The comparative degree of an adjective is used when you compare two things. The com-

parative is usually formed by adding -er to adjectives of
one syllable (great*er*, small*er*) and by placing the word
more in front of adjectives of more than one syllable (*more*
useful, *more* salable). Exception: Two-syllable adjectives
ending in -*y* may also add -*er*: *lazier* or *more lazy, angrier*
or *more angry, lovelier* or *more lovely.*

NOTE: Do not form the comparative twice:

> **WRONG:** Wai Lim is a far *more better* student than Hilda.
> **RIGHT:** Wai Lim is a far *better* student than Hilda.

3. *Superlative Degree:* The superlative degree of an adjective is used when you compare more than two things. Form the
superlative by adding -*est* to the end of a one-syllable adjective
(great*est*, proud*est*) and by placing the word *most* in front of
adjectives of more than one syllable (*most* beautiful, *most* useful). Exception: For two-syllable adjectives ending in -*y* you
may also add -*est*: for example, *laziest* or *most lazy.*

NOTE: The comparative and superlative forms of some adjectives are irregular. *Good* becomes *better* (comparative) and *best*
(superlative): *bad* becomes *worse* and *worst.* (Do not use the
superlative in place of the comparative.) The following examples illustrate the point:

> **WRONG:** Olga is the *best* of the two writers.
> **RIGHT:** Olga is the *better* of the two writers. [Use *better,*
> not *best,* if only two individuals are being compared.]

FEWER, LESS: See "*Words Often Misused: A Glossary*"
under **Wrong Word**.

adv ——————— ADVERB

Change the marked word to an adverb— usually by adding -ly.

Adverbs are words that modify (describe) verbs, adjectives, or other adverbs. Most adverbs, although far from all, are made up of adjectives with -ly endings. Adverbs limit the meanings of the words they modify by setting specific conditions such as *how* (*unusually* lucky), *when* (left *immediately*), and *where* (far *ahead*).

Certain verbs like *sing, dance,* and *write* often mislead people into using an adjective where an adverb is needed:

WRONG: He sang *beautiful.* [His song may have been beautiful, but we want to describe his action.]
RIGHT: He sang *beautifully.*

NOTE: Not all adverbs end in -ly. Some common adverbs have unusual forms—*well, rather, very late, soon, seldom, often, now, later, today, tomorrow*—and some prepositions double as adverbs: He turned *around,* fell *behind,* jumped *up.* The adverbs *well* and *very* are often incorrectly omitted in favour of adjectives:

WRONG: She writes *good.*
RIGHT: She writes *well.* [The adverb *well* specifies *how* she writes.]

WRONG: They had a *real* good time.
RIGHT: They had a *very* good time. [In careless or casual speech you often hear *real* or *really* misused as an adverb, as in a *really nice day.* A better correction than *very* nice might be a single expressive word like *wonderful.* See **Triteness.**]

AGREEMENT ———————— agr

1. **Make the verb in this sentence agree in number with its subject. If the verb is in the singular, change it to the plural, and vice versa. (See also -S Error in -S Endings.)**
2. **Make the pronoun in this sentence agree in number with its antecedent—the word the pronoun refers to.**

1. SUBJECT-VERB AGREEMENT

In the present tense, all verbs end the same in both the singular and the plural—except for the *third-person singular*, where an *-s* is added. The third-person pronouns are *he, she,* and *it*: He moves; she moves; it moves. Most of the time you will be using words that can be replaced by *he, she,* or *it*: *John* moves; *Elena* moves; *the cloud* moves. Still, the verb ends in *-s*.

All other pronouns, singular or plural, agree with the verb without the *-s*: I *work*; we *work*; you *work*. Plural words that can be replaced by the pronoun *they* also agree with the verb without the *-s*: The *machines* work.

In simple sentences you can easily see how all third-person singular subjects take or agree with *-s* verbs and how all other subjects take the form without *-s*:

- *He* always *speaks* carefully.
- Our *refrigerator makes* clanking noises. [*Refrigerator* can be replaced by *it*.]
- *They live* right under a volcano.
- *Carlyn, Ingrid, and Yuri live* very comfortably. [*Carlyn, Ingrid, and Yuri* can be replaced by *they*.]

You are likely to make mistakes in sentences when you are not sure what the subject is or when you do not know whether the subject is third-person singular or plural.

Do not be confused by words and phrases that come between the subject and verb. Find the *simple* subject (the subject stripped of all its modifying words and phrases). *The simple subject is never part of a prepositional phrase.* But prepositional phrases often follow the subject and might confuse you, as in the following sentences:

WRONG: The destruction of the world's rain forests *are* the major ecological disaster of our time.
RIGHT: The destruction of the world's rain forests *is* the major ecological disaster of our time. [The subject is *destruction,* not *forests*; the words *of the world's rain forests* constitute a prepositional phrase. You can find the simple subject if you block off, temporarily, all prepositional phrases in the sentence. See **Variety in Sentence Patterns** for definition of prepositional phrase and list of common prepositions.]

NOTE: For the present tense of the verb *to be*, all third-person singular subjects agree with the verb form *is*. All other subjects agree with *are* except, of course, for the first-person singular *I am*. (See also **-S Error in -S Endings**.)

WRONG: One of the requirements of union membership *are* monthly dues payments.
RIGHT: One of the requirements of union membership *is* monthly dues payments. [Notice that two prepositional phrases, *of the requirements* and *of union membership*, come between the subject *one* and the verb.]

In some cases, normal sentence order is reversed and the subject *follows* the verb. This can be done in order to achieve emphasis:

WRONG: After the efforts *come* the reward.
RIGHT: After the efforts *comes* the reward. [The *reward* comes.]

WRONG: There *is* two dogs in the park.
RIGHT: There *are* two dogs in the park.

Be careful of sentences beginning with *there* followed immediately by a verb. *There* will not be the subject. The subject will always follow the verb. In the above example, because *two dogs* is a plural subject, it takes the verb *are*.

When singular subjects are joined by *either... or* or *neither... nor,* use the singular verb. Remember that singular subjects are ones that can be replaced by *he, she,* or *it*; singular verbs usually end in *-s*:

> **WRONG:** Neither the mayor nor the police chief *care* to admit that the town has a drug problem.
>
> **RIGHT:** Neither the mayor nor the police chief *cares* to admit that the town has a drug problem.

If one of the subjects joined by *either... or* or *neither... nor* is not singular, then the verb agrees with the nearer subject:

> **WRONG:** Neither the captain nor the coaches *tries* very hard to win.
>
> **RIGHT:** Neither the captain nor the coaches *try* very hard to win. [*Coaches,* a *they* word, is nearer to the verb.]

> **WRONG:** Neither the coaches nor the captain *try* very hard to win.
>
> **RIGHT:** Neither the coaches nor the captain *tries* very hard to win. [The third-person singular, *captain,* is nearer to the verb; *captain* takes the singular *-s* form.]

NOTE: Collective nouns—like *group, team, family, crew, committee, couple*—are singular nouns that stand for a collection of individuals. Normally they take a singular verb: "The committee *has* adjourned," "The family *adheres* to its traditions." When, however, the focus is on the actions of the individual members within the group, and not the group in general, the noun takes a plural verb: "The family *are* quarreling with one another," "The young couple *were* exchanging kisses," "The crew *were* glad to get out of their sweaty uniforms." (Better: The crew *members* were glad to get out of their sweaty uniforms.)

2. PRONOUN-ANTECEDENT AGREEMENT

When the antecedent—the word to which a pronoun refers—is singular, use a singular pronoun. When the antecedent is plural, use a plural pronoun:

> **RIGHT:** *Tamara* knows *she* is smart. [The pronoun *she* refers to *Tamara*. *Tamara* is the antecedent, the word that the pronoun *she* refers to.]
> **RIGHT:** A short time after buying her *books*, she somehow lost *them*. [The antecedent of *them* is *books*.]

Notice that in both these examples, the pronoun agrees in number with its antecedent: *She* is singular, as is *Tamara*; *them* is plural, as is *books*.

> **WRONG:** Vacations offer us opportunities for self-renewal, but *it is* often wasted when we fail to plan ahead for *it*.
> **RIGHT:** Vacations offer us opportunities for self-renewal but *they are* often wasted when we fail to plan ahead for *them*. [*Vacations*, a plural, is the antecedent of *they*. The correction not only changes *it* to *they* but also changes the verb of the first *it* from *is* to *are*.]

> **WRONG:** I like to read a book now and then just for my own pleasure, especially if *they are* short and topical.
> **RIGHT:** I like to read a book now and then just for my own pleasure, especially if *it is* short and topical.

Writers and speakers face the problem of which pronoun to use when antecedents such as *each, everybody, everyone, anybody, nobody no one, one, either, neither* are singular. In the past, the solution has been to use the third-person singular masculine pronoun:

• Everyone in the class raised *his* hand.

However, this solution leaves out women. Several ways out of this difficulty are briefly illustrated under **Sexist Expression**, 1.

AMBIGUITY ——————— amb

Revise the ambiguous passage to make it clearly mean one thing only. Ambiguity means _double_ meaning or _vagueness_ of meaning:

AMBIGUOUS: This morning our bus was _held up_ by a pair of orange-vested men at a construction site. [Was this a _hold-up_ in the criminal sense?]
CLEAR: This morning our bus was _stopped_ by a pair of orange-vested men at a construction site.

AMBIGUOUS: Jacques asked Davinder if _he_ could help _him_. [Who needs help, Jacques or Davinder?]
CLEAR 1: Jacques asked Davinder _to help him_. [In this version, Jacques needs help.]
CLEAR 2: Jacques asked Davinder if _he needed his help_. [Here, Jacques is offering to help Davinder.]

AMBIGUOUS: Visitors sometimes leave sessions with the Premier _feeling frustrated and even a bit alarmed_. [This sentence, quoted from a news story, may leave _us_ feeling frustrated too! After all, who is feeling frustrated, the visitors or the Premier? As it stands, there are two possible answers, each shown in the clearly revised versions that follow:]
CLEAR 1: After leaving sessions with the Premier, visitors sometimes feel frustrated and even a bit alarmed.
CLEAR 2: After visitors leave sessions with the Premier, he sometimes feels frustrated and even a bit alarmed.

(See **Misplaced Modifier**; **Pronoun Reference**; and **Vagueness**.)

ap '/ ——————— APOSTROPHE

Add a missing apostrophe, or remove one you have mistakenly used. The apostrophe has three main uses:

1. It marks the possessive case of nouns.
2. It indicates a contraction.
3. It indicates plurals of letters, abbreviations, and numbers.

I. POSSESSIVE CASE OF NOUNS

For nouns, both singular and plural, that do not end in -*s*, form the possessive by adding *'s*: the *bird's* nest; the *children's* party; the *person's* name; *today's* weather.

For plural nouns that end in -*s*, add the apostrophe only: the *soldiers'* uniforms (uniforms of the soldiers); *ladies'* coats (coats for ladies); two *months'* time.

For singular nouns that end in -*s*, add *'s*. But if the last *s* would be awkward to pronounce, drop it and add only the apostrophe: the *boss's* daughter (daughter of the boss) but *The Canadian Armed Forces'* equipment, or *Harris'* leadership.

NOTE: Do not use an apostrophe in the personal pronouns *its, his, hers, ours, theirs, whose.*

2. CONTRACTIONS

Always use the apostrophe to show the omission of a letter or letters in the contracted form of words: *wasn't* (was not), *I've* (I have), *we'll* (we will), *you're* (you are), *it's* (it is), *don't* (do not).

NOTE: As a general rule, avoid contractions in formal writing.

3. PLURALS OF LETTERS, ABBREVIATIONS, AND NUMBERS

Use the apostrophe for plurals of lowercase letters: *n's, x's,* and *q's.* For capital letters you can follow either of two styles: *Qs* or *Q's*—unless the *s* alone would be confusing, such as in *As.*

Use the apostrophe for plurals of abbreviations containing periods: *B.A.'s, C.G.A.'s, R.N.A.'s.* But for abbreviations without periods you have a choice of two styles: *VIPs* or *VIP's, VCRs* or *VCR's.*

NOTE: Except in professional and academic degrees, abbreviations tend to omit periods.

You have a choice of two styles for the plurals of numbers: either *5's, 10's,* the *1900's* or *5s, 10s,* the *1900s.*

NOTE: Whenever you choose a style, use it consistently throughout your composition.

ARTICLE ———————————— art

Most problems with articles—*a, an, the*—involve either (1) use of the incorrect form of the indefinite article, or (2) use of articles with uncountable nouns.

1. Use *An* instead of *A.*

The "indefinite article" has two forms, *a* and *an.* It is used as an adjective before a noun. (The "definite article," also used as an adjective before a noun, has only one form—*the.*)

A is used before words that start with a consonant sound. *An* is used before words that start with a vowel sound. It is the sound, not the first *letter* of a word, that tells you to use *a* or *an*. For example, you write *an hour* because the *h* is silent and *hour* really begins with a vowel sound. On the other hand, you write *a once-in-a-lifetime chance* because *once* begins with a consonant sound (*w*), and you write *a union* because *union* begins with a consonant sound (*y*).

Abbreviations such as B.A. *(Bachelor of Arts)* or SASE (*self-addressed stamped envelope*—an item editors usually require of contributors to their publications) present a special problem. Does one write, "She earned *an* B.A. or *a* B.A."; "I enclose *an* SASE or *a* SASE"? Although usage is not settled on this point, common sense dictates that either may be correct, depending on how the writer wishes the reader to *pronounce* the abbreviated term.

2. In general, do not use articles before *uncountable* nouns. Remember to use articles before *countable* nouns though.

Countable nouns refer to people and things that exist as separate—and therefore *countable*—units: instructors, ostriches, coins. Use the appropriate article—*a, an,* or *the*—before such nouns:

> **INCORRECT:** I always take notes when *instructor* lectures.
> **CORRECT:** I always take notes when *the instructor* lectures.

> **INCORRECT:** Old *dog* cannot learn new tricks.
> **CORRECT:** *An* old *dog* cannot learn new tricks.

> **INCORRECT:** *Wind* blew *bouquet* out of her hand.
> **CORRECT:** *The wind* blew *the bouquet* out of her hand.

Uncountable nouns refer to things that are thought of as wholes, not as a countable set of separate units: for example, **abstractions** such as *love, progress, business*; and **substances** such as *air, water, wood, rice*.

    a. Uncountable nouns do not have *plurals*.

    b. Uncountable nouns do not normally have *articles* in front of them.

There are a number of uncountable nouns in English that do have plurals in other languages and therefore often confuse the non-native speaker of English. Examples: *advice, furniture, information, luggage, money*. (Remember, these nouns are singular and therefore take singular verbs: "Your advice *is* valuable." "Your luggage *has* arrived.")

INCORRECT: *The love*, not *the self-interest,* enables *the society* to exist.
CORRECT: *Love*, not *self-interest*, enables *society* to exist. (Abstract ideas)

INCORRECT: We had *the chicken* and *the rice* for dinner
CORRECT: We had *chicken* and *rice* for dinner. (Substances)

INCORRECT: She had *the money* to buy *the furniture* but needed *the advice* on where to purchase it.
CORRECT: She had *money* to buy *furniture* but needed *advice* on where to purchase it. (**Note:** If, in the sentence marked "incorrect," *the money* and *the furniture* are each thought of as a specific, *known* quantity or set of items, the words are not being used in their general sense as uncountable nouns. In such a case, the use of "the" would be *correct*.)

INCORRECT: He needed *the information* about where to eat well in Regina.
CORRECT: He needed *information* about where to eat well in Regina.

awk ──────────── AWKWARD

Rethink and rewrite the marked passage.

Awkward is a general term used in describing problems in writing. It may refer to one specific problem in your writing or any combination of problems. It may point simply to an error in diction (inexact use of a word) or to a much larger problem, such as the lack of coherence in a series of sentences. A similar general term is *sentence structure* (SS), which may point to anything from an obvious structural error to a messy passage requiring rewriting.

Upon analysis, some problems marked *awkward* can be given more specific names such as ambiguity, choppy sentences, mixed construction, faulty parallelism, repetition, wordiness. In using the term *awkward*, your instructor probably expects you to recognize what is wrong at a glance without more technical advice. If you see no problem with the passage marked *awk*, contact your instructor as soon as possible. If on rereading the passage you find it unsatisfactory, then use your own judgment in rewriting it. Sometimes a passage contains such a severe combination of problems that your instructor simply marks it *awk* in order not to discourage you by listing them all. In rewriting, put aside what you have originally written and focus on the original *thought* you were trying to express. Rethink your ideas as well as rewrite them. Most such problems disappear if, in revising, you make an effort to concentrate on the original *idea* you were after:

> **AWKWARD:** Due to the number of students in university, they appear to be all equal because everyone is experiences the same things.

There are several things wrong with the above sentence. Basically, the statement lacks logical coherence. In addition, the use of *due to* is an error in diction, and *is experiences* results from simple carelessness. To call this sentence *awkward* rightly points the student back to the drawing board for total rethinking and revision:

> **IMPROVED:** There are so many students in university undergoing the same experiences that, in many ways, they seem to be copies of one another.

> **AWKWARD:** Being an avid fan of country music and having a boyfriend who is a devoted rock fan provides a look at the two different types of music.

It is hard to say specifically what is wrong here. Is *being... and having...* a double subject? If so, it is plural and does not agree with the singular verb, *provides*. But *being... and having...* sounds more like a *dangling modifier* looking for a missing subject. Since the two halves of the sentence do not fit together, the problem may be *mixed construction. Awkward* is probably the best label for such an undeveloped sentence:

> **IMPROVED:** Being an avid fan of country music, and having a boyfriend who is a devoted rock fan, I get a good look at both kinds of music.

BRACKETS —————— br [/]

Add brackets, or if you have used brackets incorrectly, change to parentheses.

1. Use brackets to set off your own explanatory comments from the body of a text that you are quoting or editing:

   "Every village, every town [in Northern Canada] is the centre of an intense social and political life," says Mercredi.

If you were to use parentheses instead of brackets around *in Northern Canada*, your reader would think them to be Mercredi's words and not yours.

2. Use brackets to avoid parentheses within parentheses:

   Kafka's most extraordinary work begins with the description of a man suddenly changed into a giant beetle (*The Metamorphosis* [Original German edition Leipzig, 1915]).

cap ———————— CAPITALIZATION

Capitalize the word or words indicated, or change them to begin with a small ("lowercase") letter if you have used capitals incorrectly.

1. Capitalize proper names. These are the names of specific persons, places, things, groups, institutions, organizations: *Joe Fox*, the *St. Lawrence River*, *Keewatin College*, the *Metis*, the *United Nations*. (Capitalize *high school*, *college*, or *university* only if part of a proper name, like *Red River High School*, but not if used in a general sense: I am graduating from *university* next May.) The word *the* beginning names of organizations should not be capitalized: *the* United Nations, *the* Canadian Institute of Chartered Accountants.

   Capitalize *Mom*, *Dad*, *Father*, *Mother* when these words are the names used in referring to or directly addressing specific individuals (Hello, *Dad*. How is *Mom* doing?). Do *not* capitalize when these words are common nouns used to refer to these people as members of the whole *class* of moms and dads (Her *dad* worked hard for a living).

   Capitalize *East*, *West*, *South*, *North* when these words name specific regions (She took a job in the *East*), but do *not* capitalize when they are used as directions (Walk *east* five blocks).

2. Capitalize the first letter of every word beginning a sentence, including the first word of every quoted sentence: *He* said proudly, "*E*verything is in order."

3. In titles of books, articles, movies, plays, short stories, and poems, always capitalize the first and every word except short prepositions, coordinating conjunctions, and articles of four or fewer letters: *The Stone Angel; Much Ado About Nothing; The National; The Globe and Mail; A Prayer for My Daughter.*

CASE ————————————— case

Use the correct case of a pronoun.

Case is the form a pronoun takes when performing a certain role in a sentence. Three cases exist in English: the subjective case, the objective case, and the possessive case. (For nouns in the possessive case, see **Apostrophe**.) How do you know which case to use for a particular pronoun? That depends on your ability to recognize the subjects and objects in sentences. You probably have fewest problems with the possessive case, and those are usually spelling problems.

Many of the errors you make in *case* are carry-overs of informal speech patterns into the formal situation of writing, where a high degree of grammatical accuracy is usually expected.

In a simple sentence like "She hired him," we see the typical English sentence pattern: subject *(She)* + verb *(hired)* + direct object *(him)*. To use case correctly, use the subjective case in positions occupied by subjects and the objective case in positions occupied by objects. Two other sentence positions occupied by objects are important to note: indirect objects and objects of prepositions. Verbs may have not only direct objects but *indirect objects* as well: She gave *him (her, me, us,...)* a job. You can tell when *him* is an indirect object if you can "translate" it to mean *to him* or *for him*. She gave *him* a job equals She gave a job *to him*. Another position for objects is after prepositions *(to, for, of, by, with,* and so on). When the object of a preposition is a pronoun, it must be in the objective case: They voted for *him* and *me*; "...for *whom* the bell tolls."

CASE

PERSONAL PRONOUNS AND THEIR CASES

	Subjective	Objective	Possessive
Personal Pronouns			
First Person	I, we	me, us	my, mine
Second Person	you	you	your, yours
Third Person	he	him	his
	she	her	her, hers
	it	it	its
	they	them	their
Relative Pronoun	who	whom	whose
	whoever	whomever	

Sample Sentences Analyzed for Uses of Case

• I wrote her a letter about him, asking her several important questions. [*I* (subj.) *wrote* (vb.) *her* (ind. obj.) a *letter* (dir. obj.) *about* (prep.) *him* (obj. of prep.), asking *her* (ind. obj.) several important *questions* (dir. obj.).]

• I urged her to send me a reply with an extra copy for him. [*I* (subj.) *urged* (vb.) *her* (dir. obj.) to *send* (vb.) *me* (ind. obj.) a *reply* (dir. obj.) *with* (prep.) an extra *copy* (obj. of prep.) *for* (prep.) *him* (obj. of prep.).]

Common Case Problems

1. *The double subject*. Do not use the objective case in double subjects:

   WRONG: *Him* and Sheena rehearsed the duet.
   RIGHT: *He* and Sheena rehearsed the duet. [The subjective case *he* is correct. The test for the correct case is to drop "and Sheena." "Him... rehearsed" sounds wrong.]

2. *The double object*. Do not use the subjective case with double objects:

WRONG: Kate telephoned both Yvette and *he*.
RIGHT: Kate telephoned both Yvette and *him*. [*Him* is a direct object. The test for the correct case is to drop "both Yvette and." "Telephoned... he" sounds wrong.]

WRONG: Miguel gave her and *I* the information.
RIGHT: Miguel gave her and *me* the informafion. [*Me* is an indirect object.]

NOTE: Do not use *myself* as a way to avoid choosing between *I* and *me*. (Wrong: Miguel gave her and *myself* the information.) The pronouns *myself, himself, herself, ourselves, themselves, yourself, yourselves* are used either as reflexive pronouns (I hurt myself) or intensive pronouns—to provide emphasis (I'll do it myself. You yourselves are to blame!).

WRONG: They returned the album to Myra and I.
RIGHT: They returned the album to Myra and *me*. [*Me* is the object of a preposition.]

3. ***Pronoun + appositive as subject.*** Use the subjective case for sentences beginning with a pronoun plus an appositve in the subject position:

   WRONG: *Us* students are very practical people.
   RIGHT: *We* students are very practical people. [*Students*, part of the subject of this sentence, is an *appositive*, a noun that renames or identifies the noun or pronoun before it. If you drop the appositive *students*, you can see that "Us... are very practical" sounds wrong.]

4. ***Than/as + pronoun.*** Use the subjective case for comparisons ending with a pronoun intended as a subject:

   WRONG: Chantal skates better than *me*.
   RIGHT: Chantal skates better than *I*. [The sentence would logically continue as "Chantal skates better than *I do*" or "than I *skate*." The subjective case—*I*—is needed because

the pronoun after *than* is the subject of an elliptical, unfinished clause: *I skate.*]

AMBIGUOUS: Jaime likes football more than *me.* [Does Jaime like football more than *he likes* me, or does he like football more than *I do*? Probably the latter!]
CLEAR: Jaime likes football more than *I do.*

NOTE: If the pronoun after *than* or *as* is intended as the *object* of the omitted verb, then it should be in the objective case:

EXAMPLE: Janny likes him better than *me.* [Think of the sentence with the full elliptical clause included: "Janny likes him better than *he likes me.*]

5. **To be + subjective case.** Use the subjective case for any pronoun immediately following the verb *to be* (*am, are, is, was,* and so on):

WRONG: It was *her* who borrowed my new skis.
RIGHT: It was *she* who borrowed my new skis.

6. **Who (whoever)/whom (whomever).** In choosing between *who (whoever)* and *whom (whomever),* use *who if* the pronoun you want is the subject of its own clause. Use *whom (whomever)* if the pronoun you want is an *object* in its own clause:

EXAMPLE: *Who* spilled coffee on my diskette? [Correct. *Who* is the grammatical subject of this question.]
EXAMPLE: *Whom* do you agree with? [Correct. If you turn the sentence around, you get "You agree with *whom*?" and you can see that *whom* is the object of the preposition *with.*]

EXAMPLE: *Whom* the Gods would destroy they first make mad. [Correct. *Whom* is the object of the verb *destroy* in the clause "whom the Gods would destroy."]
EXAMPLE: She avoided *whoever* upset her. [Correct. You would expect the object of the verb *avoided* to be

whomever. It is not. The object of *avoided* is the whole clause *whoever upset her. Whoever* is correct because it acts as the *subject* of its own clause, *whoever upset her.*]

7. ***Whose/who's and its/it's.*** Do not confuse certain forms of the possessive case with contractions. *Whose* and *its* imply possession or ownership:

> **EXAMPLE:** *Whose* down parka is this?
> **EXAMPLE:** Take the parrot out of *its* cage.

Who's and *it's* are contractions and are used informally to replace *who is, it is,* and *it has*:

> **EXAMPLE:** *Who's (Who is)* the culprit responsible for this vandalism?
> **EXAMPLE:** *It's (It is)* your last chance.
> **EXAMPLE:** *It's (It has)* been a long day.

8. ***Pronoun + gerund.*** Use the possessive case for a pronoun that occurs immediately before a gerund (an *-ing* word used as a noun):

> **EXAMPLE:** She did not mind *my* having a second helping. [Correct. Do not write "*me* having."]
> **EXAMPLE:** We look forward to *your* joining us. [Correct. Do not write "*you* joining."]

> **NOTE:** For nouns in the possessive case, see **Apostrophe**.

CHOPPY SENTENCES — choppy

Revise your series of short, choppy sentences by varying your sentence patterns. Do not simply combine your sentences with *ands* or semi-colons. The result would be a series of *longer*

choppy sentences known as *stringy* sentences. If you master a variety of sentence types, your style will become much smoother:

CHOPPY: She had a very good coat. It was with her almost everywhere. It was a dark-blue woolen coat with a blue lining. It was full length and conservative looking. At one time it had a belt, but that was later lost. On the sleeves some worn spots were starting to appear. They showed how much she used it. It kept her warm on cold nights, and that was what counted most.

SMOOTH: She had a very good coat *that* she took with her almost everywhere. Conservative looking, it was a full-length, dark-blue woolen *garment* with a blue lining. *In spite of* having lost the belt, she used the coat *so much that* worn spots were starting to appear on the sleeves. *As far as she was concerned*, what counted most was that it kept her warm on cold nights.

ANALYSIS: A choppy paragraph of eight sentences is rewritten to form a much smoother paragraph of four sentences that is slightly shorter (sixty-eight words for the smoother version versus seventy-two for the choppy version) even though two new phrases have been added. The italicized words and phrases in the revised paragraph do not appear in the original. For the most part, they reveal logical relationships between thoughts, relationships that are not clearly seen in the original. To revise choppy writing, do not simply combine short sentences into longer ones but use the resources of phrasing and sentence structure *to show logical relationships between thoughts*. The main techniques of revision used above are discussed in detail under **Subordination**; **Transitions**; and **Variety in Sentence Patterns**.

COHERENCE ———————— coh

Completely rewrite the indicated passage. As it now stands, the material does not make clear, logical sense. The parts are not organized in a logical pattern.

Coherence literally means "holding together." Other words for coherence are *organization, order, arrangement,* and *pattern.* When your phrases, sentences, and ideas hold together, your writing has coherence. In coherent writing, the train of thought is easy to follow. Connections and relationships between ideas are clear. Major ideas stand out from minor points, and ideas of equal importance receive equal emphasis.

LOGICAL ORDER OF IDEAS: Simply throwing down your ideas as they occur to you does not guarantee coherence. The mind very often leaps ahead of the pen, so give your pen or your typing fingers time to catch up and arrange your thoughts in a logical sequence. Developing and working from an outline will help you to establish a logical order to your ideas. One idea should lead clearly to the next in an orderly, step-by-step pattern with no missing links.

There should be an obvious reason that your third sentence follows the second, not vice versa.

LINKAGE ORDER OF IDEAS: A good writer uses various devices to clarify the relationships *between* ideas. A good writer provides links or transitions that lead the reader from sentence to sentence without confusion. Consider the links—the italicized words—between the following two sentences:

Walking is a fast-growing sport. *In fact,* there is a new sports magazine on the market this month *that devotes the entire issue to walking.*

In fact is a transition between the two sentences, a logical bridge telling the reader that factual evidence is at hand to support the first statement. The clause *that devotes the entire issue to walking* links the two sentences by repeating the main idea of the first sentence, including the key word *walking*. Without these two devices you would have the following *incoherent* piece of writing:

> Walking is a fast-growing sport. There is a new sports magazine on the market this month.

There are four main ways to link ideas:

1. Transitional words or phrases. [See **Transitions**.]
2. Repetition of key words or ideas. [See **Repetition**.]
3. Pronouns. [See **Pronoun Reference**.]
4. Demonstrative adjectives. [See **Adjective**.]

1. TRANSITIONAL WORDS OR PHRASES

EXAMPLE: More than a hundred pairs of peregrine falcons have bred successfully on city office towers. *As a result*, the chance of their extinction seems remote. [*As a result* is a transitional phrase showing the logical connection between the two sentences. Among commonly used transitions are *for example, however, consequently, first of all, on the other hand*. See **Transitions**.]

2. REPETITION OF KEY WORDS OR IDEAS

EXAMPLE: Most people agree that inflation is caused by *declining productivity* of workers and businesses. It is *declining productivity*, not the national debt, that threatens the economy of our country.

EXAMPLE: *Overpopulation* is one of the root causes of political problems. *Too many people* demanding too few resources is a problem of global dimensions. [*Too many people* repeats the idea of *overpopulation*.]

3. PRONOUNS

EXAMPLE: Mrs. Gauci gave the assignment last week. *She* emphasized that *it* would be due today. [Both *she* and *it* are pronouns that refer to nouns in the previous sentence.]

4. DEMONSTRATIVE ADJECTIVES

EXAMPLE: The jury reached a decision in less than twenty minutes. *This* verdict would affect the defendant for the next twenty years. [Demonstrative adjectives point back to previous ideas. There are four demonstrative adjectives: *this, that, these, those.*]

Passage Lacking Coherence

Some people feel that public schools have the right to ban certain books from their libraries. <u>Huckleberry Finn</u> has been banned off and on ever since its publication. <u>The Diviners</u> is often banned. This is, in other people's opinion, a violation of freedom of speech.

The Above Passage Revised

(*Note:* Added linking devices are in italic type.)

Some people feel that public schools have the right to ban certain books from their libraries. *For example,* <u>Huckleberry Finn</u> has been banned off and on ever since its publication. Another book often banned is <u>The Diviners</u>. *Such a banning of books* is in other people's opinion a violation of freedom of speech. [*For example* is a transitional phrase; *such* is a pronoun; and *banning of books* is a repetition of key words.]

col :/ ─────────── COLON

Place the colon after an introductory statement to call attention to what follows, such as in the following:

1. **An explanation.**
2. **A list of items.**
3. **A long quotation.**

1. COLON BEFORE AN EXPLANATION

An explanatory *word* or *phrase* following a statement may be set off with either a colon or a dash:

> **WRONG:** The quality of the food served in the cafeteria may be described in a single word as: revolting!
> **RIGHT:** The quality of the food served in the cafeteria may be described in a single word: revolting!
> **RIGHT:** The quality of the food served in the cafeteria may be described in a single word—revolting!

If you use *as*, you do not need the colon. *As*, like the colon, points to the explanatory *revolting*. *As*, however, does not dramatically stop the flow of the sentence the way the colon or the dash does.

Generally, the longer the explanatory passage, the more suitable it is to introduce it with a colon:

> **INAPPROPRIATE:** Small businesses must be protected through appropriate governmental action—the effective and thorough enforcement of combines legislation in order to maintain competition and prevent agreements and combinations destructive to business. [In a formal style, the colon is *preferred* but not absolutely *required*.]

RIGHT: Small businesses must be protected through appropriate governmental action: the effective and thorough enforcement of combines legislation in order to maintain competition and prevent agreements and combinations destructive to business.

When a full sentence follows a colon, you may capitalize the first word or not, as you please:

RIGHT: Here is our honest opinion: *We* think you are an exceptional student.
RIGHT: Here is our honest opinion: *we* think you are an exceptional student.

If a *quoted* sentence follows the colon, you *must* begin the sentence with a capital letter:

WRONG: The sign was perfectly clear: "*no* smoking in this section."
RIGHT: The sign was perfectly clear: "*No* smoking in this section."

If you are quoting a passage that does *not* begin with a capital letter, do not supply one:

WRONG: She had several choice descriptions of the speech: "Wobbling," "waffling," and "wordy" were the mildest.
RIGHT: She had several choice descriptions of the speech: "wobbling," "waffling," and "wordy" were the mildest.

NOTE: If you use the words *the following* or *as follows*, expect to place a colon after them:

RIGHT: When I study I proceed *as follows*: First, I review the underlined passages in my textbook; then I accurately copy all technical words and write brief definitions for them.

NOTE: Do not place a colon after the words *as* or *such as* or the forms of the verb *to be* (*is*, *are*, and so on).

> **WRONG:** Her salads include items *such as*: lettuce, tomatoes, carrots, and chick peas.
> **RIGHT:** Her salads include items such as lettuce, tomatoes, carrots, and chick peas.

> **WRONG:** The virtues my parents instilled in me are: patience, tolerance, and charity.
> **RIGHT:** The virtues my parents instilled in me are patience, tolerance, and charity.

2. COLON BEFORE A LIST OF ITEMS

Use a colon to introduce a series of items at the end of your sentence:

> **WRONG:** On a long ocean voyage be sure to take *along*: plenty of books, a deck of cards, a chess set, and a warm blanket.
> **RIGHT:** Be sure to take the following things with you on a long ocean voyage: plenty of books, a deck of cards, a chess set, and a warm blanket.

There is no natural pause after *along*, as there is after *voyage* in the previous example. Do not use the colon to interrupt the normal flow of the sentence. In other words, a colon must be preceded by a complete main (independent) clause:

> **WRONG:** The items to take with you on a long ocean voyage *are*: plenty of books, a deck of cards, a chess set, and a warm blanket. [The colon after *are* is not needed and interrupts the flow of the sentence.]
> **RIGHT:** On a long ocean voyage be sure to take *along* plenty of books, a deck of cards, a chess set, and a warm blanket.

RIGHT: The items to take with you on a long ocean voyage *are* plenty of books, a deck of cards, a chess set, and a warm blanket.

WRONG: On a long ocean voyage take along items *such as*: plenty of books, a deck of cards, a chess set, and a warm blanket. [Do not use a colon after *as* or *such as*.]

RIGHT: On a long ocean voyage take along items *such as* plenty of books, a deck of cards, a chess set, and a warm blanket. [No punctuation is needed after *such as*.]

3. COLON BEFORE A LONG QUOTATION

If you are quoting a long passage, especially one that consists of two or more sentences, introduce it with a colon, not with a comma:

In "Politics and the English Language," George Orwell writes: "A scrupulous writer, in every sentence that he writes, will ask himself at least four questions, thus: What am I trying to say? What words will express it? What image or idiom will make it clear? Is this image fresh enough to have an effect? And he will probably ask himself two more: Could I have put it more shortly? Have I said anything that is avoidably ugly?"

COMMA ——————————— c ,/

1. **Insert a comma before a coordinating conjunction that connects two main (or independent) clauses. *And, but, nor, for, or, so,* and *yet* are coordinating conjunctions.**

2. **Insert a comma after sentence parts that come before the main clause, especially long phrases and subordinate clauses.**

3. **Set off parenthetical (nonrestrictive) sentence parts with commas.**

4. **Insert commas between words, phrases, and clauses in a series.**

5. **Use a comma to separate coordinate adjectives.**

6. **Do not use unnecessary commas.**

The following six instructions for using the comma will solve practically all your comma problems:

1. *Use the comma before coordinating conjunctions* (and, but, nor, for, or, so, *and* yet) *that join two main clauses.*

• The instructor encouraged her students to ask questions in class, *and* she noted that those who did were often the ones who did best on her exams.

• He thought he would be snapped up by a major corporation, *but* he finally settled for anything he could get.

   EXCEPTION: If the main clauses are very short, you do not have to separate them with a comma:

• I never had *and* I never will.

2. *Use the comma after sentence elements that appear before the main clause, such as subordinate clauses and phrases.*

• *When the instructor spoke to the student*, she asked him whether he studied very much.

The words in italics are a subordinate clause. [The term is defined under **Variety in Sentence Patterns**.]

- *Shaking his head*, the student replied that his roommates kept the television set blaring day and night.

- *As a solution to the problem*, the instructor recommended the temporary removal of a few parts from the set.

  EXCEPTION: Most short prepositional phrases that come before a main clause are not followed by a comma:

- *After a moment* the student admitted that television wasn't his only distraction from studying.

Certain introductory words and phrases, like *for example, in short, in fact, however,* and *consequently*, are used to form a bridge, or transition, from one sentence to another and are followed by a comma:

- *In short*, the student admitted that he simply disliked the course. [See **Transitions**.]

NOTE: If a subordinate clause *follows* the main clause, normally you do *not* separate them with a comma:

- No fishing boats went out that day because the water was too rough. [No comma between *day* and the subordinate clause beginning with *because*.]

However, modern usage is flexible. Read your sentence aloud. If you hear a definite *pause* between the main and subordinate clauses, you may separate them with a comma:

- I knew he deserved his punishment, although I admit I did feel a moment of pity for him.

3. *Use commas to set off parenthetical sentence elements.*

  NONRESTRICTIVE ELEMENTS: A sentence element is parenthetical, or *nonrestrictive*, if it supplies information that is not essential to the clear meaning of the sentence. In the following examples, the nonrestrictive elements are italicized:

• Modern automobiles, *which are smaller and more fuel efficient than ever*, strike me as more practical and attractive than the older gas guzzlers.

• She is, *I agree*, a good sport.

• Soil erosion, *the loss of water-storing topsoil*, turns land into desert.

To test whether an element is parenthetical, remove it from the sentence. If the basic idea of the sentence remains the same, then the element which you have removed is parenthetical and should be set off with commas. Read the above examples without the words in italics, and you will find that the ideas of the original sentences remain unchanged.

RESTRICTIVE ELEMENTS: Restrictive sentence elements are necessary to the meaning, as in this example:

• Everyone who is hard of hearing should wear a hearing aid.

Notice that the clause *who is hard of hearing* is essential to the meaning of the sentence. If you remove it, the basic idea of the sentence is distorted. Restrictive elements are not set off from the rest of the sentence by commas.

4. *Use commas between items in a series.* A series is made up of three or more elements, which may be single *words*, *phrases*, or *clauses* (these last three italicized words are in a series):

• The basement was *dark*, *damp*, and *cold*.

The formula for items in a series is *a*, *b*, and *c*. Also acceptable in formal writing is the formula *a*, *b* and *c*, where there is no comma between the last two items in the series: The basement was *dark*, *damp* and *cold*. Whichever form you choose, try to use it consistently throughout a piece of writing.

- He stumbled across the room, down the stairs, and through the doorway. (A series of three prepositional phrases.)

- I came, I saw, I conquered. [Three main clauses, if they are very short, may be connected in a series by commas.]

- To ease the housing shortage, we need to know *what measures we can take, how we can fund them, and who can get the job done most efficiently.*

5. *Use commas between coordinate adjectives that come before a noun.* Coordinate adjectives are adjectives that stand in *equal* relation to the noun they modify:

- She is an *old, faithful* servant.

- Look at his *clear, twinkling* eyes.

The test for coordinate adjectives is to insert the word *and* between them and omit the comma. If the adjectives are coordinate (equal in rank), you will feel no awkwardness: *clear and twinkling* eyes.

The test shows that the following examples are not coordinate adjectives: a *small living* room, a *little old* man. The second adjective in each pair is really treated as part of the noun. It would be awkward to say *a small and living room* or *a little and old man*. Where you can insert the *and*, use the comma. Where you cannot insert the *and*, omit the comma.

NOTE: For the use of commas with quotation marks, see **Quotation Marks**.

6. **Do not use unnecessary commas.** If you use *too many* commas, you will probably find your types of errors discussed below.

a. Do not use commas to separate subjects from verbs and verbs from their objects or complements—unless nonrestrictive elements come between them. (For "restrictive" and "nonrestrictive" elements see 3 above.)

ERROR: (Comma between subject and verb): The cat-and-mouse game between clever computer criminals and harassed security experts, threatens never to end. [The simple subject is *game*. Its verb is *threatens*. No comma should separate them. The long phrase *between... experts* is restrictive, that is, essential to defining the subject, and therefore should not be set off by a comma on *either* end.]

ERROR: (Comma between verb and its complement): For me, the basic ingredients of a good spaghetti sauce are, fresh garlic cloves and an extra virgin olive oil. [The comma after the verb *are* is not needed.]

b. Do not use commas to separate restrictive elements from the rest of the sentence. (See 3 above.)

ERROR: Paul Ehrlich's book, *The Population Explosion*, warns humankind against overburdening the "carrying capacity" of the planet. [The phrase *The Population Explosion* is restrictive, that is, essential to the meaning of the sentence, and should not be set off by commas. Commas here imply that this is Ehrlich's *only* book. If it were, then the book's title would be parenthetical or nonessential information. But Ehrlich has written many books, not just this one. The sentence should therefore read: "Paul Ehrlich's book *The Population Explosion* warns..."]

c. Do not use a comma before a parenthesis.

> **ERROR:** We put new locks on our doors, (in spite of the cost) for fear of burglary. [Omit comma after *doors*.]

d. Do not use a comma between adjectives if you cannot smoothly insert the word *and* between those adjectives instead. (See the discussion of "coordinate adjectives" in 5 above.)

> **ERROR:** They discovered an ancient, Egyptian tomb. [You cannot smoothly write "an ancient *and* Egyptian tomb." Therefore you cannot use a comma between these adjectives either.]
> **ERROR:** He was a funny, little fellow. [Omit the comma.]

e. Do not use a comma after the last item in a series. (See 4 above for the correct use of commas *between* items in a series.)

> **ERROR:** Many computer researchers feel that terms such as telepresence, artificial reality, and immersive simulation, are preferable to the more commonly used "virtual reality." [The comma after *immersive simulation*, the last in a list of three items, should be omitted.]
> **ERROR:** Gold, silver, and platinum, tend to have widely varying market values. [Omit the comma after *platinum*.]

f. Do not use a comma before the *and* of a compound predicate.

> **ERROR:** Science fiction is becoming more popular, and is increasingly being regarded as worthy of serious literary study. [Omit the comma before *and*. If the subject *it* came after *and*, the comma would be correct, according to comma rule 1 above, in which the comma is used "before coordinating conjunctions that join two main clauses." In this example *and* is connecting only the predicate part of

a sentence—the verb-part left when a subject is missing—
to the predicate part of the whole main clause in front of
it. In other words, *and* is just joining the two parts of a
compound predicate, and therefore no comma should go
before it.]

ERROR: Unemployment has been widespread, and has
not been so severe since the Great Depression of the 1930s.
[Omit the comma after *widespread.*]

g. Do not use a comma with a question mark or an exclamation
point.

ERROR: "Are you coming to the party?," she asked. [Omit
comma after *party?*]
ERROR: Fresh fruit!, he thought, already smelling the
apples. [Omit comma after *fruit!*]

h. Do not use a comma after *and, but, or, nor, for, yet, so.*

ERROR: The house was lovely, but, it was too big for us.
[Omit comma after *but.*]
ERROR: I knew it was wrong, yet, I was tempted to do it.
[Omit comma after *yet.*]

CS ——————— COMMA SPLICE

**Change the comma to a period or to a
semicolon. Do not join, or splice, two separate
sentences with a comma. The comma splice, a
type of run-on sentence, prevents readers from
distinguishing between the end of one thought
and the beginning of the next:**

COMMA SPLICE: Toronto is a busy industrial city,
thousands of cars and trucks move through it every day.

REVISION I: Toronto is a busy industrial city. Thousands of cars and trucks move through it every day.

This first revision changes the comma splice to two sentences by changing the comma after *city* to a period and capitalizing *thousands.* You could also correct the error by changing the comma after city to a semicolon:

REVISION 2: Toronto is a busy industrial *city; thousands* of cars and trucks move through it every day. (Before substituting a semicolon, be certain how to use it. See **Semicolon.**)

NOTE: To avoid splicing two separate sentences with a comma, learn to recognize what makes up a separate sentence. At the heart of a sentence are a *subject* and a *verb.* (In the example just given, *Toronto* is the subject of the first sentence, and *is* is the verb.) To test further for a sentence, say your group of words out loud. If it *sounds like a complete statement* (and has a subject and a verb), it is likely to be a *sentence.*

A second type of comma splice occurs in sentences beginning with words (called *conjunctive adverbs* when they link main clauses) such as *therefore, however, then, nevertheless, moreover, also, still, thus,* or with expressions such as *in fact, for example, that is, on the other hand, in other words.* These are transitional words or phrases that begin a new main clause or a new sentence. Most often the main clause beginning with such an expression should be linked with the previous main clause by a semicolon:

COMMA SPLICE: We packed all our luggage, then we were on our way to the airport.
REVISION: We packed all our luggage; then we were on our way to the airport. [Changing the comma after *luggage* to a semicolon removes the comma splice.]

COMMA SPLICE: He was an excellent computer programmer, however, he frequently failed to show up for work.

REVISION: He was an excellent computer programmer; however, he frequently failed to show up for work.

NOTE: Sometimes a conjunctive adverb is *not* found at the beginning of its clause. In such a case, *do not* set it off with a semicolon:

WRONG: He was an excellent computer programmer. *Frequently; however,* he failed to show up for work.
RIGHT: He was an excellent computer programmer. *Frequently, however,* he failed to show up for work. [In such cases, as this example shows, it is also best to separate the two main clauses with a period rather than a semicolon.]

COMMA SPLICE: I have always loved sports, in fact, I was once the youngest member of my bantam hockey team. [Place a semicolon after *sports*.]
REVISION: I have always loved sports; in fact, I was once the youngest member of my bantam hockey team.

comp ——————— COMPARISON

Add the word or words needed to complete the comparison. Incomplete comparisons lead to absurd or illogical statements. (For the irregular comparative forms of *good* and *bad*, see Adjective, 2.)

ILLOGICAL: The traffic in Vancouver is worse than Edmonton. [*Traffic* is illogically compared to a city!]
REVISED: The traffic in Vancouver is worse than *the traffic* in Edmonton.
BETTER: The traffic in Vancouver is worse than *that* in Edmonton. [Use a pronoun to avoid awkward repetition.]

ILLOGICAL: In this poem Earl Birney expresses ideas differently from most other poets. [*Ideas* are illogically compared to *poets*.]
REVISED: In this poem Earl Birney expresses ideas differently from *those of* most other poets.

INCOMPLETE: The auditor's income was as high, if not higher than, the company's president's. [The complete phrase should be *as high as*.]
REVISED: The auditor's income was as high *as*, if not higher than, the company's president's.

INCOMPLETE: Gordie Howe *has* had a longer career than *any* player in the major leagues.
REVISED: Gordie Howe has had a longer career than *any other* player in the major leagues.

INCOMPLETE: Luis received a higher score than *anyone* in the class.
REVISED: Luis received a higher score than *anyone else* in the class.

DANGLING MODIFIER — dmod

1. **Change the dangling element into a subordinate clause by adding a subject and verb.**

2. **Change the main clause so that the subject is correctly modified by the dangling modifier.**
   (See also *Misplaced Modifier*.)

The modifier in your sentence *dangles* because it does not clearly and logically relate to another word in the sentence. Use either one of the above changes to revise the sentence:

DANGLING: *When sitting*, my shoulders tend to slouch back. [*I*, the logical subject of the modifier, does not appear in the sentence. As now written, the sentence says that *my shoulders* are sitting.]

REVISION 1: *When I sit*, my shoulders tend to slouch back. [This revision changes the dangling elements into a subordinate clause.]

REVISION 2: When sitting, *I* find that my shoulders tend to slouch back. [This revision makes the subject of the main clause, *I*, agree with the dangling element.]

Note that the introductory phrase should logically modify the noun or pronoun *immediately following the comma*. Further, that noun or pronoun should always be the *subject* of the main clause.

DANGLING: *To type well*, your legs must be in the correct position. [Are *your legs* doing the typing?]

REVISION 1: *If you want to type well*, your legs must be in the correct position.

REVISION 2: To type well, *you must keep* your legs in the correct position.

REVISION 3: To type well, *keep* your legs in the correct position. [In imperatives—statements giving commands—the subject pronoun *you* is implied.]

DANGLING: *Going home*, it started to drizzle. [Where is the subject who is *going*?]

REVISION 1: *As I was going home*, it started to drizzle.

REVISION 2: Going home, *I felt it starting* to drizzle.

DANGLING: *Fearful of a threatened lawsuit*, his decision to pay me back was wise.

REVISION: Fearful of a threatened lawsuit, *he wisely decided* to pay me back. [*He*, not *his decision*, was fearful.]

DANGLING: *At the age of three*, my mother discovered I had a speech impediment. [Was the mother *really* three when she discovered this?]

REVISION: *When I was three,* my mother discovered I had a speech impediment. [In this case, there is simply no *smooth* way of revising that keeps the dangling phrase *At the age of three* unchanged.]

DASH ─────────────── dash —/

Insert or delete a dash.

Use the dash to mark an abrupt shift in thought, to emphasize a parenthetical element, or to ensure a clear reading. However, using the dash too frequently for emphasis becomes monotonous. For the most part, avoid using the dash if commas or parentheses will serve equally well.(See **Emphasis**.)

NOTE: Most computer keyboards are equipped with only a hyphen and not a dash. To type the dash, use two strokes of the hyphen key [--]. Leave no space before or after the dash. (See **Colon**, 1.)

Examples of the proper use of the dash:

• "I would like—no, as a matter of fact, I wouldn't." [Abrupt shift in thought.]

• "I must admit—since you force me to tell you—that my opinion of you is not very high." [Dashes set off a parenthetical element emphatically. Parentheses muffle and make unemphatic the material they enclose.]

• Intel Corporation's powerful new Pentium computer chip was discovered to harbour a bug—a tiny programming defect. [A dash may be used to introduce a brief explanation, but see **Colon**, 1.]

dic —————————— DICTION

Change the word or phrase you have used to one that is more exact in *meaning*, to one that is less *wordy*, or to one that is more suited in tone to the rest of your essay.

Certain errors in diction (word choice) recur frequently. Check to see if your error is dealt with in "*Words Often Misused: A Glossary*" that appears at the end of this book (under **Wrong Word**). In any case, the following suggestions are a guide for correcting and avoiding mistakes in diction:

1. Check the exact meaning of the word you have used in a large modern dictionary ("college-edition" size, at least). You may find in some cases that your problem is spelling, as, for example, confusing *accept* with *except*. This and other common spelling errors are treated in "*Words Often Misused: A Glossary*" (under **Wrong Word**).

2. See a sample list of common wordy expressions under **Wordiness**.

3. Sometimes the word you choose does not fit the *tone* of the rest of your essay. Tone is the attitude the writer takes toward the subject. The tone may be solemn, humorous, conciliatory, angry, informal, technical. It may reflect any emotional or intellectual attitude. In a formal essay, for example, it would not be suitable to use terms like *guy, mom, dad,* or *dude*, but these may be appropriate in an informal letter.

   Good dictionaries give a variety of labels to words. Check your dictionary to see whether the word you have used is labeled as slang, regional, technical, informal, or nonstandard. Nonstandard words are out of place in the formal style of standard written English that is generally expected of you. If the particular usage of a word is *standard* (generally acceptable in formal speaking and writing), it will not be labeled. Some words may have different labels for different meanings: For example, a word like *cool* could have one definition with a standard meaning and another definition with a slang application. (See **Slang** and **Jargon**.)

DOCUMENTATION ———— doc

Use the correct style of documentation in your writing for both in-text citations and bibliography.

The purpose of documentation in writing is to give your readers the opportunity to trace your ideas back to their original sources. It is used to acknowledge the material that you have drawn from external sources. While you may use ideas from various sources in unique ways, you need to identify the sources of the ideas. Using ideas, information, or actual language from external sources without acknowledging it is plagiarism or intellectual theft.

Each academic discipline uses a form of documentation in its papers. The most common ones are the Modern Language Association (MLA) style, which is used for documentation in languages and literature, and the American Psychological Association (APA) style, which is used in the humanities. Each of these require that sources are documented within the text of your essay, and acknowledged in full at the end of your essay. Some other disciplines, such as science, engineering, or medicine, have other documentation styles but, for most college students, MLA and APA are the most common.

NOTE: Footnotes are rarely used in documenting sources. Footnotes are used to add material that would otherwise interfere with the flow of your writing.

There are handbooks for each of these styles available through your college or university library or bookstore. While this section highlights each of these styles, you should acquaint yourself with the handbooks and use them when doubts or questions arise. This section will give you examples of MLA and APA citations for a book, a magazine article, and a World Wide Web site.

The Works Cited List (MLA style) or References (APA style) come at the end of the essay as your complete bibliography. It should list all books, articles, films, radio and television programs, electronic communications, and even interviews that you have consulted and to which you have referred in your writing.

MLA CITATIONS

1. In-Text Citations

Provide readers with enough information so that, when they refer to your list of Works Cited at the end of your writing, they can identify the correct document. A typical in-text citation is made up of the last name of the author and the page on which the idea can be found.

> **EXAMPLE:** People living by themselves make up over 20 percent of all Canadian households and over 10 percent of all adults (Teevan, 179).

NOTE: Notice that the in-text citation is in parentheses and is part of the sentence. Punctuation follows the citation.

2. Works Cited List, Examples

Think about citations as a series of sentences, each of which ends in a period. Each sentence contains specific information: the *author*, the *title*, or the *publication information*.

Last, first name   title and sub-title, underlined

Teevan, James. <u>Basic Sociology: A Canadian Introduction</u>,
    4th ed. Scarborough: Prentice Hall, 1993.

Publication information

a) A Book

Teevan, James. <u>Basic Sociology: A Canadian Introduction</u>,
    4th ed. Scarborough: Prentice Hall, 1993.

b) An Article in a Magazine

Harris, Catherine. "How Stock Markets Behave." <u>Canadian
    Banker</u> July/August 1996: 38.

c) A World Wide Web Site

Sharma, Saed. "Selling on the Web: The Virtual Mall."
    On-line. Available World Wide Web: http://www.
    wimsey.com/Duluthie/.

APA CITATIONS

1. In-Text Citations

A typical reference is made up of the author's last name and
the year of publication. Page references are rarely included
unless you are quoting directly.

> People living by themselves make up over 20 percent
> of all Canadian households and over 10 percent of all
> adults (Teevan, 1993).

2. Works Cited List, Examples

Last, first name date   title and sub-title
         | |

Teevan, James (1993). <u>Basic Sociology: A Canadian Introduction</u>, 4th ed. <underline>. Scarborough: Prentice Hall.
                                   |
                          Publication information

a) A Book

Teevan, James (1993). <u>Basic Sociology: A Canadian Introduction</u>, 4th ed. <underline>. Scarborough: Prentice Hall.

b) An Article in a Magazine

Harris, Catherine (1996). "How Stock Markets Behave." <u>Canadian Banker</u> July/August, 38.

c) A World Wide Web Site

Sharma, Saed (1996). "Selling on the Web: The Virtual Mall." [On-line] Available World Wide Web: http://www.wimsey.com/Duluthie/.

CBE Citations

1. In-text citations

The Council of Biology Editors provides two alternatives for in-text citations. The first is a name-year parenthetical approach similar to that used in APA. The second is a numbered system which refers to the Reference List. If you use the name-year parenthetical approach, your Reference List will be organized alphabetically. If you use the numbered approach, your Reference List will be organized by the order of works cited in the body of your text.

Boyle's Law states that the volume of a given amount of gas held at constant temperature varies inversely with the pressure (Holum, 1994).

Holum[1] states that Boyle's Law says that the volume of a given amount of gas held at constant temperature varies inversely with the pressure.

Whichever style of in-text documentation you use, remember to be consistent.

2. Works Cited List, Examples

title and sub-title:
Last, first name   capitalize first word

Holum, John R. Fundamentals of general, organic, and bio-logical chemistry. <no underline> Toronto: John Wiley and Sons, Inc.: 1994. 800 p.

Publication Information

a) A Book

1. Hawking, S.W. Black holes and baby universes and other essays. New York: Bantam Books; 1993. 320 p.

b) An Article

1. Weissman, I.L., Cooper, M.E. How the immune system develops. Sci Am 1993 Mar; 269(3): 65–71

Provide your reader with both the volume number (269 in this case) and the issue number (3 in this example). Follow this with the page numbers of the article.

c) A World Wide Web Site

With any electronic resource, start with a statement of the type of resource and then give the information you would give for the print version. End with the date that you accessed the resource.

WWW.Silicon Graphics.Digital imaging for the movies. http://www.saabusa.com; Feb. 1997.

ED ERROR
-ed error ——— IN -ED ENDINGS

Add -ed to indicate the past tense of the verb.

Often the past-tense -ed ending is not clearly heard in spoken English. Thus, it is easy to omit it in writing. Examples:

OMITTED: *I hope* she would be there. [In many cases, of course, only the *d* is omitted rather than the full -*ed*.]
CORRECTED: *I hoped* she would be there. [The -*ed* ending sounds like a *t*. A *t* may be hard to hear right after a *p*. The same is true for the -*ed* after the *k* in *asked* or after the *sh* in *wished*. No wonder you can easily omit it in writing.]

OMITTED: She *try* to telephone him.
CORRECTED: She *tried* to telephone him. [It is easy not to hear the *d* sound in *tried* right before the *t* in *to*. As to the spelling rule, note that verbs ending in a *consonant* plus *y*—*hurry* and *empty* for example—change their *y* to an *i* and add either -*es* for the present tense or -*ed* for the past: *hurries, hurried, empties, emptied*. Notice, however, that verbs that end in a *vowel* plus *y* undergo no such change: *play, plays, played*.]

There are three exceptions to this *ay*-verb rule: *Lay, pay* and *say* regularly become *lays, pays,* and *says* in the present but change to *laid, paid,* and *said* in the past.

> **OMITTED:** *I use* to live in Nova Scotia.
> **CORRECTED:** *I used* to live in Nova Scotia. [This is the most common error of this type. The *-ed* in *used* sounds much like a *t* and is not easy to hear before the *t* in *to*. The same is true for *suppose to*, which should be *supposed to*.]

NOTE: Do not drop the tense endings from past participles used as adjectives:

• The church boasted ornate, *stain*-glass windows. [Change "stain-glass" to "stained-glass"]

ELLIPSIS ———————————— ell .../

In formal writing, the ellipsis—three double-spaced periods—is used only to show that you have omitted material from a *quoted* passage. Do not use the ellipsis as a substitute for the dash or parenthesis.

Examples of the formal use of the ellipsis are as follows:

> Poetry turns all things to loveliness, it exalts the beauty of that which is most beautiful, and it adds beauty to that which is most deformed:... it subdues to union... all irreconcilable things.
> —Percy Bysshe Shelley

Use *four* double-spaced periods in the ellipsis when the material you have omitted ends a sentence:

> Then the door of the cabin was flung wide open and a strange figure stepped across its threshold. The figure was that of an old, old

man.... In his hand was an instrument resembling a flute. [The following was omitted from the second sentence: "...with white hair hanging around loosely about his stooping shoulders."]

em ——————————— EMPHASIS

Give proper emphasis to the more important parts of the sentence and less emphasis to the less important parts.

Use the following methods for emphasizing important words or ideas.

1. *Rearrange your sentence to give the important words and phrases their proper emphasis.* The position of greatest emphasis is the *end* of your sentence. Next in emphasis is the beginning of your sentence:

   POOR EMPHASIS: We jammed into the car and started on our trip *in the morning, just after the sun rose.* [The italicized phrases are the least important elements of the sentence, but they are placed at the end, the position of most emphasis.]
   PROPER EMPHASIS: In the morning, just after the sun rose, we jammed into the car and started on our trip. [The main clause, beginning we *jammed*, is now properly emphasized.]

2. *Change the weak passive voice of the verb to the strong active voice.* (See **Voice.**)

   UNEMPHATIC PASSIVE VOICE: At camp, many games *were played by the children* that were not played at home.
   EMPHATIC ACTIVE VOICE: At camp, *the children played* many games that they did not play at home.

3. ***Underline a word or phrase for strong emphasis.*** Use sparingly. Underlined words in a manuscript appear in italics *(slanted type like this)* in print. Underline a word or phrase for strong emphasis only if you cannot achieve the emphasis by rephrasing or rearranging sentence parts. (See **Italics**.)

It is of course *possible* that all or any of our beliefs may be mistaken.... But we cannot have reason to reject a belief except on the ground of some other belief.

—Bertrand Russell

EXCLAMATION POINT ——————— excl !/

Insert an exclamation point, or omit one if you have used one incorrectly. The exclamation point is used to express *strong* feeling. Do not overuse it.

PROPER USE: What a wonderful, wonderful day! [Excitement.]
PROPER USE: Get out of here! [A strong command.]

OVERUSE: The first baseman leaped up! He snatched the ball out of the air! The double play that followed was easy!
REVISION: The first baseman leaped up. He snatched the ball out of the air. The double play that followed was easy. [These short, jabbing sentences are emphatic enough without exclamation points.]

FRAGMENTARY
frag ——————————— SENTENCE

Change the sentence fragment to a complete sentence.

You have written only a phrase or a subordinate clause, or some other *piece* of a sentence, but not a full sentence. If you can logically attach what you have written to the previous or the following sentence, do so. If not, expand your fragment into a full sentence by adding the missing element(s).

In certain types of creative writing, fragments are used effectively to suggest the frequently rapid and nongrammatical flow of thought, especially at emotional high points. But in formal, expository writing, where logic and calm are needed, sentence fragments are rarely appropriate.

The simplest sorts of fragments to correct are called *period faults*. They are sentences ended *too soon*. Usually a comma is needed in place of the faulty period. In the following examples, unjustifiable sentence fragments are in italics:

PERIOD FAULT: I do not have the steadiest hand in the world. *As you can see from my writing.*

The fragment is a subordinate clause that should be attached to the previous sentence by a comma. (For a further explanation, see **Comma**, 3.)

REVISION: I do not have the steadiest hand in the world, *as you can see from my writing.*

PERIOD FAULT: He spent some of his university years in Vancouver. *A city whose weather is warm eight months of the year.*

The fragment is an appositive. An *appositive* is a noun that renames or identifies a previous noun. In this case, the appositive *city* refers to the already named *Vancouver*. Join the appositive to the first part of the sentence with a comma.

REVISION: He spent some of his university years in Vancouver, *a city whose weather is warm eight months of the year.*

In more complicated cases, fragments result when parts of a sentence are missing altogether:

FRAGMENT: She lectured on a number of occult subjects. *For example, about numerology.*

The fragment is a phrase. It is better style to make a complete sentence out of it than to add it to the previous sentence.

REVISION: She lectured on a number of occult subjects. For example, *she spoke* about numerology.

Better yet, however, would be to recast the entire idea: *She lectured on numerology and a number of other occult subjects.*

FRAGMENT: John would not make a good captain. *A good player, yes, but not always a good sport.*

The fragment here is a sentence part that needs a subject and verb. But the subject and verb were both omitted. Supply them:

REVISION: John would not make a good captain. *He is* a good player, yes, but not always a good sport.

HYPHEN ———————————— hy -/

Insert a hyphen (-) where indicated.

The hyphen is mainly used to connect words that are to be regarded as a unit of meaning: *fire-eater, helter-skelter, rabble-rouser.* (In many cases, usage is not generally agreed upon even among dictionaries. In order to be consistent, choose one current dictionary and follow it.)

HYPHEN

The following examples illustrate special uses of hyphens, such as preventing misreading and end-of-line word division.

1. Use a hyphen to connect modifying words before a noun when such words act as a unit of meaning:

- *an intelligent-looking face*
- *nineteenth-century history* [but not in *the history of the nineteenth century*]
- *a do-or-die attitude*
- *behind-the-scenes dealing* [But in the sentence "There were shady dealings going on behind the scenes," no hyphens are used because *behind the scenes* comes *after* the noun.]
- *four-, and six-cylinder cars.* [Sometimes hyphens are *suspended* in a series before a noun.]

2. Use a hyphen to prevent misreading:

- *a foreign-car dealer* [Unless you mean *a foreign car-dealer*— a visiting American, for example, who sells cars in her native New York.]
- *a small-appliance store* [Such a store could be very large, indeed, but nobody would believe it if you removed the hyphen!]
- They *re-covered* the chair. [Compare: They *recovered* the stolen chair.]
- I could think of one *more-expensive* gift to buy. [Compare: I could think of one *more expensive* gift to buy. (Here, "one more expensive gift" means one *additional* expensive gift.) The hyphenated example simply *compares* the cost of two gifts. The version without the hyphen means that *all* the gifts are in and of themselves expensive!]

3. Use hyphens for numbers between twenty and one hundred: *twenty-nine, sixty-two, eighty-eight.* (See **Numbers.**)

4. Use a hyphen for an end-of-line word division: *hyphen-ation,* not *hyphe-nation.* Divide words at the end of a full

syllable. Follow the word divisions in a good dictionary, for example: sym-pa-the-tic.

(See also **Dash.**)

IDIOM——————————————————— id

Use an acceptable idiomatic expression.

An idiomatic expression, or idiom, is a linguistic form that occurs in one specific language and will not usually be found in any others. English is a language so rich in idioms that both native speakers of English and non-native speakers often misuse such expressions.

In English there are two areas that present problems involving idiomatic usage: (1) vocabulary, and (2) grammatical structure.

1. *Vocabulary.* Many expressions may seem illogical or nonsensical in the contexts in which they occur. Take the following sentence, for example: "She made money hand over fist." A native speaker is unlikely to have a problem with this remark, but a non-native speaker may not know that "to make money" means to *earn* money (not to manufacture it), and that to make money *hand over fist* means to make *lots* of money. Or take this sentence: "The fool wasted ten years before he came to his senses." The phrase *to come to (one's) senses*—finally to act more wisely—is immediately clear to most native speakers, but may not *make sense* (another idiom!) to a non-native speaker.

Standard versus nonstandard idioms: Many idioms are perfectly acceptable in formal written usage as standard English, but there are many also that are *slang*, or *nonstandard*, and are labeled as such in any good dictionary. Use a desk-size college English dictionary (or a bilingual one, if preferable) to be sure of how an idiom is used, and write down idioms that you hear and find confusing. (For specific help with vocabulary, see also the brief sections in this book on **Diction**, **Jargon**, **Sexist Expression**, **Slang**, and **Triteness**, and read the Glossary under **Wrong Word**.)

2. *Grammatical Structure.* The idiomatic nature of English is not confined to matters of vocabulary but extends to grammatical structures as well. Some of the major problems related to *grammatical* usage are found in this handbook in the sections **Article**, **Case**, **-Ed Error**, **Voice**, **-S Error**, and **Tense**.

inc ——————— INCOMPLETE CONSTRUCTION

Add the word or words necessary to complete the construction that you now have.

PREPOSITION OMITTED: She was greatly interested and enthusiastic about the project.
REVISED: She was greatly interested *in* and enthusiastic about the project.

VERB OMITTED: The people were all interesting, and my vacation, in general, wonderful.
REVISED: The people were all interesting, and my vacation, in general, *was* wonderful. [The plural verb *were*, used with *people*, does not agree with the singular noun *vacation*.]

VERB OMITTED: We never have and never shall attack without provocation.
REVISED: We never have *attacked* and never shall attack without provocation. [The auxiliary verb *have* must be followed by *attacked*.]

RELATIVE PRONOUN OMITTED: He thinks that I am nasty and I can hardly wait to insult him.

REVISED: He thinks that I am nasty and that I can hardly wait to insult him. [What a difference a *that* makes! See a similar example under **Parallelism**.]

NOTE: See **Comparison** for other examples of incomplete constructions.

ITALICS ——————————— ital

Underline the word or passages indicated. If you are using a word processor, use the italic feature.

When printed, underlined words appear in italic or slanted type, *like this*. If you underline or italicize words, you are asking the reader to pay greater-than-usual attention to them. Frequent underlining for the purpose of emphasis may backfire, however, for it will no longer seem to signal what is unusual. Underline no more than is absolutely necessary—under normal circumstances, perhaps three or four times per page at most. There are four situations that call for underlining:

1. Underline the titles of books, magazines, newspapers, plays, and movies. Do not put quotation marks around them: *Neuromancer, Maclean's, The Globe and Mail, Phantom of the Opera, Due South.* (For further information see **Quotation Marks,** 3.)

2. Underline foreign words and expressions: *coup d'etat, al fresco, chutzpah, persona non grata, intifada.*

3. Underline words or letters if they are not used for their meaning, but as words or letters only.

    EXAMPLE: Add a *u* to *gaze* and you get *gauze*.

4. Underline words when strong emphasis is desired: "I'm leaving *now*," she declared, "*not* tomorrow!" (See **Emphasis**.)

NOTE: Do not underline and do not put quotation marks around the title of your own essay or composition.

jarg ——————————————— JARGON

Do not use jargon, the highly technical language of professions and specialized interest groups, if you are writing for a general audience.

> **JARGON:** Digging in a long-buried *insula* in the old Roman camp, we uncovered a shard-filled *midden*.
> **REWRITTEN:** Digging in a long-buried *block of buildings* in the old Roman camp, we uncovered a shard-filled *heap of ancient refuse*. [In this version, the archeological terminology of the original is "translated" for the average reader.]

> **JARGON:** When I bit into the chocolate bar, I had an instant of *parageusia* and was sure that someone had spiked it with salt.
> **REWRITTEN:** When I bit into the chocolate bar, I had *a taste hallucination* for an instant and was sure that someone had spiked it with salt. [There's no need for the fancy psychological vocabulary.]

list ——————————————— LISTS

Use lists to achieve emphasis by breaking up complex statements and allowing main ideas to stand out. (See also *Emphasis, Parallelism*.)

Listing can be an effective way to highlight a sequence or a group of important, related points. But in constructing a list, you still need to be grammatically correct. As such, a list needs an appropriate introduction. A list is essentially a part of a sentence and is used to visually show equal relationships. Structurally, each element in the list should use the same grammatical constuction and punctuation.

There are two types of lists that you may use.

ORDERED LISTS

In an ordered list, each element follows the preceding one in sequence or in importance. Typically, the list will be numbered to indicate the order.

EXAMPLE: There are a series of steps to completing the requirements for a Certified General Accountant designation through this college. These are the following:

1. completing the six-credit Business Studies Certificate;
2. completing the twelve-credit Accounting Certificate;
3. completing the twenty-credit Accounting Diploma; and
4. passing the accrediting examinations.

NOTE: Notice that each element of the list starts with the same construction, and the first three elements end with the same punctuation. An appropriate transition is used in the third element (See **Transitions**) and the list ends with a period, indicating the end of the sentence.

NON-ORDERED LISTS

In a non-ordered list, the sequence is unimportant. Instead of using numbers, use bullets to indicate each element.

EXAMPLE: In the first semester of your Accounting Diploma, you should take the following subjects:

- English,
- Introduction to Business,
- Introduction to Accounting,
- Introduction to Marketing,
- Computers and Business Information Systems, and
- Business Statistics.

(See also **Colon, Semicolon, Comma.**)

log ———————————————— LOGIC

Reread the marked passage and try to discover the flaw in your language or line of reasoning.

You may have failed to argue your point convincingly. Your problem may be ineffective phrasing, ineffective thinking, or both. Think through your idea again, and if it still seems worth defending, try to present it more effectively.

Many of the problems in writing that damage your logic—the clear and convincing expression of your ideas—are dealt with in this handbook under the following headings: **Abstract Expressions; Ambiguity; Coherence; Incomplete Construction; Mixed Construction; Paragraph; Point of View; Transitions; Vagueness**.

If the problem lies mainly in the *thought* rather than in the expression, perhaps your difficulty falls into one of the following common categories of faulty logic:

1. Oversimplification

2. Overgeneralization

3. Appeal to authority

4. Appeal to emotion

5. Non sequitur

I. OVERSIMPLIFICATION
log/simp

When you oversimplify, you make a statement that you want your readers to believe, but you give either inadequate evidence or too simple an explanation. Few statements can be absolutely proved, but you should present *good evidence* or *sound argument* to support your point of view. Good evidence consists of concrete examples and relevant facts and figures. A sound argument recognizes and tries to deal with the complexity of most issues:

EVIDENCE MISSING: The quality of student life on campus is poor. If conditions do not improve soon, many students may leave this college. [If no examples of the poor conditions that are claimed are given, the reader has no way of judging how true that first statement might be. Supply the evidence.]

IMPROVED (EVIDENCE SUPPLIED): The quality of student life on campus is poor. *In a recent student survey, 70 per cent of those polled found the food at the student cafeteria unacceptable, and 62 per cent found the library staff "unhelpful".* If conditions do not improve soon, the recently announced tuition increase may drive many students away from this college.

COMPLEXITY UNRECOGNIZED: If families were more stable, no real drug problems would exist in this country. [This is an example of overly simple cause-and-effect reasoning. It is too simple to asssume that unstable family conditions *directly* cause drug problems. A revised statement would avoid such cause-and-effect arguments.]

IMPROVED: The instability of the family unit is a *factor that contributes* to the drug problem in this country.

2. OVERGENERALIZATION
log/gen

You overgeneralize when you allow *no exceptions* to your statement. Other than in the natural sciences, it is almost impossible to find general statements that apply to absolutely every known case. Learn to *qualify* (to admit and allow for exceptions) your statements. Be careful of using words like *always, never, all, none*:

> **OVERGENERALIZATION:** College students are interested in partying first, studying last. [Use qualifying words such as *some, many, sometimes, often*. As this statement stands, *college students* implies *all* college students without exception.]
>
> **IMPROVED:** *Many* college students are interested in partying first, studying last.

3. APPEAL TO AUTHORITY
log/auth

In appeal to authority, you offer no stronger backing for your point of view than the word of a presumed authority on the subject. The word of established, well-recognized authorities may be good support for what we believe. However, there are problems with relying on *false* authorities. The star goalie of the Stanley Cup final is not necessarily the best authority on what beer to drink. In addition, even the best authorities sometimes contradict one another. What you should avoid, if at all possible, is relying on authority and nothing but authority for your beliefs:

> **APPEAL TO AUTHORITY:** Jogging is one of the best exercises for ensuring good health and a long life. The Premier's personal physician recently said so to reporters. [The social status of this politically connected physician has evidently impressed this writer tremendously. Surely

there must be better evidence to be found for the benefits of jogging.]

IMPROVED: *Recently published evidence that joggers have a lower incidence of cardiac problems leads me to believe that* jogging is one of the best exercises for ensuring good health and a long life.

APPEAL TO AUTHORITY: Earth landings of flying saucers with alien beings in them have actually occurred, according to last week's *National Investigator*, and the government has for many years been suppressing news of them. [Suppose the *National Investigator* is a periodical that is not known for objective, factual reporting. Although the statement *may* be true, the *authority* quoted in support of it will prevent most readers from giving it serious consideration.]

IMPROVED: *There are many unconfirmed reports that* Earth landings of flying saucers with alien beings in them have actually occurred, *and it is possible that* the government has for many years been suppressing news of them. [There is nothing wrong with making the most outrageous statements, as long as you properly *qualify* them—as the words *unconfirmed* and *possible* help to do.]

4. APPEAL TO EMOTION
log/emot

In appeal to emotion, instead of using objective evidence and rational argument, you support your views by an appeal to your readers' emotions—to their prejudices, fears, or vanities:

APPEAL TO EMOTION: Why would anyone want Hickman as president of the university? He has twice been divorced, and his present wife is an alcoholic. [An appeal to many people's prejudices is substituted for an examination of Hickman's administrative credentials.]

IMPROVED: Why would anyone want Hickman as president of the university? *As we all remember, he was* *dismissed several years ago from his position as financial vice-president.*

APPEAL TO EMOTION: As almost any leading corporate executive will tell you, a Sears suit is the only kind worth buying. [The appeal here is to the reader's desire for success and status and not necessarily to the quality of the suit itself.]

IMPROVED: *Although the price is high*, I prefer Sears suits to *any others because of the excellent material and craftsmanship that go into them.*

5. NON SEQUITUR
log/ns

The Latin term *non sequitur* means *it does not follow. You move* from one thought to another as if there were a logical connection between them, but there is none. (*Appeal to emotion* is a special case of *non sequitur.*) When one thought does not follow another, the reason may be, very simply, that you were hasty and left out a necessary bridge or transition. If you supply the transitional thought, the reader clearly sees the connection between the other two thoughts:

NON SEQUITUR: Because my next high school was much larger, we were allowed a longer lunch hour. [Something is missing here. What is the connection between the size of the school and the length of the lunch hour?]

IMPROVED: Because my next high school was much larger, *and the lines in the crowded cafeteria moved more slowly*, we were allowed a longer lunch hour.

(See **Coherence**.)

NON SEQUITUR: Because of an all-male student body, in class each student could be himself and act and speak naturally. [This is a very jumbled and misleading statement because at least two facts or ideas are left out.]

IMPROVED: Because the student body *at my high school was all male, showing off for the females was strictly an after-school distraction*, and in class each student could be himself and act and speak naturally.

MISPLACED MODIFIER —————— mm mod

Put the misplaced word or phrase in a closer or clearer relation to the word it modifies. (See also *Dangling Modifier*)

A *modifier* is a word or group of words that adds descriptive detail to any of four types of words in a sentence: nouns, verbs, adjectives, and adverbs. In the sentence, "He loves old cars," *old* is an adjective that modifies, or describes, the noun *car*. In the sentence "They fought bravely," *bravely* is an adverb that modifies the verb *fought*. In the sentence, "Be very careful," *very* is an adverb that modifies the adjective *careful*. Sometimes a modifier is *misplaced*. It shows up too late in a sentence to connect unmistakably with the word it modifies. In such cases confusion may result, as in the following examples:

MISPLACED: They *only* wanted to steal what they needed. [Does the writer mean, "They would get what they needed *only through stealing*"? This is unlikely. The writer probably means, "They wanted to steal no more than they needed." The proper placement of *only* can bring out exactly this meaning.]

CLEARER: They wanted to steal *only* what they needed.

MISPLACED: The emperor was just and kind to people *in his way*. [This sounds like the emperor was kind to people who were obstacles in his path.]

CLEARER: *In his way,* the emperor was just and kind to his people.

MISPLACED: He fell while he was running *into a manhole*.
CLEARER: He fell *into a manhole* while he was running.

MISPLACED: The woman who was working *quickly* swallowed her lunch. [This is a case of a *squinting* modifier, one that can modify either of two words. Does *quickly* modify *working* or *swallowed*? Most probably it modifies *swallowed*. See also **Ambiguity**.]
CLEARER: The woman who was working swallowed her lunch *quickly*.

mx — MIXED CONSTRUCTION

Change one part of the sentence to make it match the rest.

Your sentence begins with one construction or figure of speech, then shifts to another that cannot logically or structurally complete the sentence:

MIXED SENTENCE PARTS: By throwing the upper-right-hand lever is the way to stop the machine.

The two halves of this sentence do not fit together. The first part is an adverbial phrase that cannot serve as the subject. The second part, beginning with *is*, needs a noun as a subject. To correct the sentence, give it a subject in one of the following ways:

CORRECTION I: *Throwing* the upper-right-hand lever *is* the way to stop the machine. [Leave out the *By*; then the first clause becomes a noun phrase and the subject of the verb *is*.]

CORRECTION 2: By throwing the upper-right-hand lever, *you can* stop the machine. [Change *is the way to* to *you can*. Now *you* is the subject of the sentence, and the adverbial clause *By throwing...* modifies the verb *can stop*.]

MIXED SENTENCE PARTS: *The reason* so few professors seek employment at this university *is because* we are located so far from any major urban centre. [*Because* begins an adverbial clause that many writers wrongly put to work as a *noun*. Change the adverbial clause to a noun clause. *The reason... is because* becomes *The reason... is that*.]
CORRECTION: *The reason* so few professors seek employment at this university *is that* we are located so far from any major urban centre. (See also *Reason is because* in "*Words Often Misused: A Glossary*" under **Wrong Word**.)

MIXED SENTENCE PARTS: *Just because* she is rich is no reason to suppose she is happy.

This sentence has the same type of error as the previous one, except in reverse. This typical *just because* sentence forces an adverb clause—*because she is rich*—to serve as the subject. Subjects ought to be nouns, noun clauses, or other types of *noun* constructions. The simplest correction changes the adverbial clause into a noun clause: *Just because* becomes *The simple fact that* or *The mere fact that*.

CORRECTION: *The mere fact that* she is rich is no reason to suppose she is happy.

MIXED SENTENCE PARTS: Now, and not next month, is *when* we should write letters to our legislators.

The *is when* and *is because* constructions are similar: adverbs are forced to do the job of nouns. Correct most *is when* sentences simply by striking out *is when* and switching the two halves of the sentence around.

NUMBERS

CORRECTION: We should write letters to our legislators now, and not next month.

MIXED METAPHORS: The *wheels* of fate moved their grimy *hands*. [Do *wheels* have *hands*? As you can see, mixing metaphors (figures of speech) can result in an absurd image—funny, but not intentionally so.]

MIXED METAPHORS: A *tongue of* land jutted out from the *foot* of the cliff. [It is absurd to imagine a *foot* sticking out its *tongue*.]

num ——————————— NUMBERS

1. Spell out any figure that can be spoken in one or two words: *thirty, fifty-five, three hundred, two million.* [NOTE: Hyphenate numbers between twenty and one *hundred: forty-two, seventy-one, ninety-six.*]
2. Use numerals for any sum that must be expressed in three or more words: *172,307, 1002.*

EXCEPTION: Spell out figures that begin a sentence: *Three hundred sixty-eight* students work part-time.

¶ ——————————— PARAGRAPH

Begin a new paragraph at the place marked.

In most writing, the first line of a paragraph is *indented*, that is, begins several spaces to the right of where a line usually begins. In some cases, paragraphs can be indicated by blank lines between blocks of types or by introductory symbols such as an asterisk (*), bullet (•), or number.

The beginning of each new paragraph marks a new stage in the development of your essay. Just as sentences are the largest subunits of a paragraph, so paragraphs are the largest subunits of your essay. In formal writing, a paragraph does not begin and end just anywhere. The main idea, or topic, of an essay needs to be developed in each of its important *aspects*, and a new paragraph signals the shift to a new aspect of the discussion. (If your topic is broad enough and your essay long enough, each of the main aspects may be broken down into two or more sections, or paragraphs.) If, for example, you were writing a short essay on the types of teachers you have known and you ended up writing about five specific types, you might decide to write an introductory paragraph briefly mentioning your purpose and the five types you will treat. Then, you would probably devote *one paragraph* to a description (with examples) of *each type*. Your essay would, therefore, be divided into at least six paragraphs.

The main idea of each paragraph is usually found in one sentence called the *topic sentence*. (The theme of the whole essay is usually found in the first paragraph and is called the *thesis statement*.) A paragraph consists of a topic sentence, or main idea, plus a number of sentences that *develop* that main idea in some satisfactory way through a *logical argument*, or a series of *details* or *examples*, or any combination of these methods. The topic sentence is usually the first one in a paragraph, although it sometimes appears at the end, as a summary of details or examples that come before it.

There are three main organizational features to a well-structured paragraph:

1. *Unity*, the relevance of all sentences to the topic sentence. The avoidance of digressions—wandering from the paragraph topic.

2. *Development*, elaboration of the main idea with enough details, examples, arguments, and so forth to give the impression of full or adequate treatment.

3. *Coherence*, the connection between one sentence and the next in a logical pattern.

PARAGRAPH

The use of linking devices is an essential means of achieving coherence. There are four main types of linking devices:

1. Transitional words or phrases
2. Repetition of key words or ideas
3. Pronouns
4. Demonstrative adjectives (*this, that, these, those*)

(For more information see **Coherence, Transitions, Thesis,** and **Topic Sentence.**)

> **EXAMPLE: One of the most significant changes in Canadian family lifestyles in recent years has been the increase in the number of working women.** [*Topic sentence*] Each year more and more are joining the ranks of the employed in search of personal fulfillment and financial independence. *In fact,* [*Transitional Phrase*] over half of the adult female population is now in *the labour force.* [*Repetition of key idea*] *Of particular importance to the family lifestyle* [Repetition of key words] is the fact that half of all children under eighteen now have working mothers. Statistics Canada reported that 45 per cent of all *mothers* [*Rep. key word*] of preschool children are presently working. *That* [*Demonstrative adjective*] *figure* [*Rep. idea*] is four times higher than it was just thirty years ago.
>
> *This increase in the number of working women has caused a redefinition of family roles.* [*Transitional sentence linking paragraphs*] **One important change is that husbands and children are expected to do more around the house.** [*Topic sentence*] In many households *children are expected not only to do* [*Rep. key idea*] the dishes and clean their rooms, but also to do the family grocery shopping, cook some of the meals, and help care for the younger children. *And because a working woman contributes to the family's economic welfare,* [*Rep. key idea*] husbands are increasingly sharing in what was once considered "woman's work": caring for the children, cooking, and doing the laundry.

PARALLELISM ——————— paral //

When two or more sentence elements are equally important in content and function, make them alike in grammatical form.

Parallelism is the matching of sentence elements with one another: subject with subject, verb with verb, object with object, modifier with modifier. Usually, when these like sentence elements appear in a pair or a series, they are connected with coordinating conjunctions:

> **POOR:** I enjoy going to movies, listening to music, and cards.
> **REVISION I:** I enjoy *going* to movies, *listening* to music, and *playing* cards.

The verb is *enjoy,* and its objects are *going, listening,* and *playing.* Because these sentence elements are all objects, they should be in the same form. In this case the objects should all be gerunds: *-ing* words used as nouns.

> **REVISION 2:** I enjoy *movies, music,* and *cards.*

This series is also parallel because the three objects—movies, music, and cards—are all nouns. However, these nouns are not as specific as the gerunds in the first revised sentence.

> **POOR:** The opinion of one newspaper columnist is that the member of parliament has lied to the voters, and we should therefore throw him out of office.
> **REVISED:** The opinion of one newspaper columnist is *that* the member of parliament has lied to the voters and *that* we should therefore throw him out of office.

The second *that* makes it clear that the opinion that follows is solely the columnist's and does not belong to the writer of the sentence. You see how important clear parallelism can be.

PARENTHESES

POOR: She plays the piano with ease, with confidence, and takes pleasure in it.
REVISED: She plays the piano *with ease*, *with confidence*, and *with pleasure*.

In the revised sentence we have a series of parallel prepositional phrases. Because the three phrases modify the same verb—*plays*—they should be parallel.

paren ( ) / ———— PARENTHESES

Use parentheses to enclose material that is clearly additional commentary or detail and is not essential to the meaning of the sentence.

Whatever is enclosed in parentheses appears relatively unimportant to the reader. Use parentheses sparingly; never use them when you can use commas instead.

Effective Use of Parentheses

• I walked right up to him (no one was with him at the time) and told him what we had decided.

• Last week she came up with a brilliant new idea (the seeds of it had been germinating in her mind for months) only to see it rejected as absurd by the committee.

Ineffective Use of Parentheses

• His brother told him (Paolo) not to annoy him (Faisel) any more.

You should not compensate for poor reference of pronouns by using explanatory parentheses. The sentence needs rewriting

74

to achieve a smooth style and clear meaning: *His brother told Paolo not to annoy Faisel anymore.*

- Some critics think that atmospheric pollution (not the population explosion) is the more serious challenge to human survival.

Commas are better than parentheses to set off this relatively important part of the sentence.

NOTE: Do not place a comma before a parenthesis: I had eaten too much, (two breakfasts that day!) and felt guilty about flouting my diet. [Omit comma after *much*.]

POINT OF VIEW ———— pov

1. **Make the pronouns in your sentences agree in *number* and *person*.**
2. **Make the verbs in your sentences agree in *tense*, *mood*, and *voice*.**
3. **Do not carelessly present as your own statements those that should be attributed to others.**

I. PRONOUN SHIFTS

Avoid Shifts in Number

A shift in pronoun number occurs when you shift between singular and plural pronouns while referring to the same noun:

SHIFT: During the sixties, women gained more control over their roles in society than they had previously possessed. Now is no time for *her* to give up *her* struggle for equal rights.

REVISED: During the sixties, women gained more control over their roles in society than they previously possessed. Now is no time for *them* to give up *their* struggle for equal rights. (See **Agreement,** 2.)

Avoid Shifts in Person

The personal pronouns are classified as *first-*, *second-*, and *third-person* pronouns (singular or plural). (See **Case.**) Examples of first-person pronouns are *I, me, we, our.* Second-person pronouns include *you, your, yours.* Among the more common third-person pronouns are *he, she, it, one, they.* Avoid needless shifts in person not only within the same sentence but also from sentence to sentence and from paragraph to paragraph throughout the entire essay:

SHIFT: If *one* stops to watch them work, *you* are greeted with a smile.
REVISION: If *one* stops to watch them work, *one* is greeted with a smile. [Avoid frequent use of the impersonal *one.* It can make your style seem stiff.]
REVISION 2: If *you* stop to watch them work, *you* are greeted with a smile.

2. VERB SHIFTS

Avoid Shifts in Tense

A verb's tense tells your reader when the action takes place. (See **Tense.**) If you shift unnecessarily, for instance, from the past to the present, you may confuse your reader. Avoid unnecessary shifts in tense not only within the same sentence but also from sentence to sentence and from paragraph to paragraph throughout an essay:

SHIFT: He *rushed* to catch his train but *misses* it by half a minute. [A needless shift from the past—*rushed* —to the present—*misses*.)

REVISED: He *rushed* to catch his train but *missed* it by half a minute.

Avoid Shifts in Mood

Engish has three verb moods: the *indicative*, the *imperative* and the *subjunctive*. Most of the time, we speak and write in the indicative mood—the verb forms used for making declarative statements such as "I work on weekends." We use the imperative mood when we issue commands (to an implied subject, *you*): "*Work* faster." The most common mood-shift *error* is from the imperative to the indicative:

> **SHIFT:** *Be* sure to visit the science exhibition, and then you *should go* to the art show. [*Be* is the imperative; *should go* is the indicative.]
> **REVISED:** *Be* sure to visit the science exhibition, and then *go* to the art show. [Both verbs, *be* and *go*, are now in the imperative mood.]

Occasionally, we use the *subjunctive* mood—when we discuss possibilities instead of facts and when we use certain cliché phrases like "*Be* that as it may." Of the very few uses of the subjunctive in English, here is a typical one—proposing a condition contrary to fact—involving the use of the past tense of the verb "to be":

> **INCORRECT:** If Pierre Berton was actually a group of authors, I could understand his enormous productivity.
> **CORRECT:** If Pierre Berton were actually a group of authors, I could understand his enormous productivity.

Avoid Shifts in Voice

Avoid changing from the active voice to the passive voice when your subject is still active. (See **Voice**.) Often there is no need to change the subject from clause to clause within the same sentence:

SHIFT: *We* predicted the results more easily after the *margin of error* had been reduced. [Who reduced the margin of error?]

REVISED: *We* predicted the results more easily after we had reduced the margin of error.

3. SHIFTS IN THE ATTRIBUTION OF STATEMENTS

Be Clear About Who Is Saying What

Make sure that when you present the thoughts of others, the reader cannot take them as your own statements or opinions. Only a few words are needed for clarification:

SHIFT: In Eudora Welty's "Petrified Man," women are portrayed as victims of Hollywood-inspired fantasy. *The real men in their lives are all hindrances, millstones, and rapists.* [The italicized sentence appears to be the opinion of the student who wrote this passage.]

REVISED: In Eudora Welty's "Petrified Man," women are portrayed as victims of Hollywood-inspired fantasy. *The female characters feel that* the real men in their lives are all hindrances, millstones, and rapists. [Addition of the italicized words makes it clear that the opinion that follows is not the student's own but belongs to the characters in Welty's story.]

pro—— PRONOUN REFERENCE

Make the pronoun you have used refer clearly to a previous noun (its antecedent).

I. DANGLING PRONOUNS

Some pronouns, particularly *which*, *this*, and *it* can *dangle* in a sentence because they simply have no antecedent—no obvious noun—to which they can refer. A dangling pronoun error usually happens when writing imitates the informality of ordinary speech. Often, these pronouns try to refer to a whole previous idea, but the idea has not been written in the form of a noun. To revise the idea, restate it in the form of a noun:

UNCLEAR REFERENCE: He felt extremely angry toward her, which made it difficult for him to speak to her.

The dangling pronoun *which* is used to refer to the whole preceding main clause. It lacks a specific antecedent, a noun to which it refers. Revise the idea in either of two ways:

1. Change the *which* part of the sentence to fit the main clause.
2. Change the main clause to fit the *which* part of the sentence.

REVISION 1: He felt extremely angry toward her. *His attitude* made it difficult for him to speak to her. [This solution turns one sentence into two.]

REVISION 2: His anger toward her reached a *peak* that made it difficult for him to speak to her. [*That* now clearly refers to the noun *peak*.]

UNCLEAR REFERENCE: Jie played varsity football, chaired the history club, spoke fluent Mandarin, and drew cartoons for the college newspaper. This explains why the student body elected him president.

The pronoun *this* is forced to refer to the whole preceding sentence. To revise, combine the pronoun *this* with a noun, or perhaps a more descriptive noun phrase, that sums up the ideas of the whole previous sentence:

REVISION: Jie played varsity football, chaired the history club, spoke fluent Mandarin, and drew cartoons for the college newspaper. This record of all-round excellence explains why the student body elected him president.

UNCLEAR REFERENCE: How can you not be happy to see *the leaves appear* in the spring and the difference *it* makes in everything around you? [The pronoun *it* awkwardly refers to the whole previous clause, *the leaves appear in the spring.*]

REVISION: How can you not be happy to see the leaves in the spring and the difference their appearance makes in everything around you? [Sometimes, through rewriting, you can elimate a pronoun-reference problem simply by getting rid of the troublesome pronoun—*it*, in this case.

UNCLEAR REFERENCE: *It said* in last week's newspaper that the North American Free Trade Agreement could aggravate the present recession.

Similar to this kind of sentence is the one that begins *They said on the radio that...* The *it*—or *they*—implies a subject that is not stated. In formal writing, avoid this kind of construction. A simple revision uses *I read* or *I heard* to begin such a sentence.

REVISION: *I read* in last week's newspaper that the North American Free Trade Agreement could aggravate the present recession.

BETTER: Last week's newspaper reported that the North American Free Trade Agreement could aggravate the present recession.

2. AMBIGUOUS PRONOUNS

Some pronouns refer *ambiguously* to either of two previous nouns. Pronouns should clearly refer to one noun and one noun only. Your job is to remove the ambiguity. Reduce your pronoun's workload to one noun to which it clearly refers. (See **Ambiguity**.)

AMBIGUOUS REFERENCE: When Kamal spoke to Peter, he said he doubted that he would be invited to the party. [Does the last *he* refer to Kamal or Peter?]

REVISION: When Kamal spoke to Peter, he said, "I doubt that I will be invited to the party." [The use of direct quotation is the simplest way to solve this sort of reference problem.]

AMBIGUOUS REFERENCE: Even if the salesperson persuades you to purchase an item, do not sign anything. Ask her to leave the contract with you so that you and your spouse may read it thoroughly. If *she* will not *do it*, show her the door. [In the last sentence, the ambiguous use of *she* and *it* can lead to a rather amusing interpretation.]

REVISION: Even if the salesperson persuades you to purchase an item, do not sign anything. Ask her to leave the contract with you so that you and your spouse may read it thoroughly. If the *salesperson* will not *leave it with you*, show her the door [It is not enough to change *she* to *salesperson*. The dangling *it* in *do it* has no noun to which it refers. It is made to refer to either of two verb-object combinations: *leave the contract* or *read it*. To clarify this, change *do it* to *leave it with you*.]

QUESTION MARK ———— QM ?/

Do not omit the question mark or use it unnecessarily.

NOTE: Your instructor may use this symbol not to point out a punctuation error but to question the logic, clarity, or factual precision of a passage.

Use a question mark only after a *direct* question.

ERROR: "Will you take out the garbage," he requested. [Replace the comma after *garbage* with a question mark.]
ERROR: Would I ever succeed, I asked myself. [Replace the comma after *succeed* with a question mark.]

QUOTATION MARKS

Do not use a question mark after an *indirect* (or reported) question.

> **ERROR:** He asked me to take out the garbage? [Replace the question mark with a period. This is not a *direct* question but a report about a question.]
>
> **ERROR:** I asked myself if I would ever succeed? [Replace the question mark with a period. Note that if a *direct* question followed "I asked myself," it would be "Would I ever succeed?"]

quot "/" — QUOTATION MARKS

Use quotation marks to set off the following:

1. **directly quoted words,**
2. **words used in an unusual way, and**
3. **the titles of subunits of a book or magazine—a chapter, story, poem, and so on.**

WHEN TO USE QUOTATION MARKS

1. *Use quotation marks to enclose a passage of directly quoted words:*

- The flight attendant said, "Fasten your seat belts, please."

- In his *Essay on Criticism*, Alexander Pope writes, "A little learning is a dangerous thing...."

> **CAUTION 1:** Do not use quotation marks for *indirect* quotations. An indirect quotation is a second-hand report of what someone said, and it is often introduced by the word *that*:

MISUSE: My brother said that "he was unhappy about the outcome."
REVISION: My brother said that he was unhappy about the outcome. [Remove the quotation marks. Quotation marks could be used around the words in this sentence that are quoted: My brother said that he was "unhappy about the outcome." Or a complete direct quotation could be used: My brother said, "*I am* unhappy about the outcome."]

CAUTION 2: In quoted dialogue, start a new paragraph with every change in speaker:
CLUTTERED: "Do you realize," she said, "that we'll next be seeing each other on Friday the thirteenth?" "Do you think I'm superstitious, Lisa?" he said. "Of course not, Hedda, but what made you shudder like that?"
REVISED: "Do you realize," she said, "that we'll next be seeing each other on Friday the thirteenth?"

"Do you think I'm superstitious, Lisa?"

"Of course not, Hedda, but what made you shudder like that?"

Keep identification of the speaker, such as *he said* or *she said*, outside of the quotation marks:

- "I suppose," *she remarked*, "that success comes only with time." [Because the quoted passage is one complete sentence, the interrupting words are set off by commas and not followed by a period or semicolon.]

- "I understand the plan," *Subashin said*. "I think it might work." [In this case, two separate sentences are quoted. *Subashin said* must be followed by a period, for it marks the end of one quoted sentence.]

When quoting long prose passages (five lines or more), do not use quotation marks. Instead, indent the entire passage five spaces to the right (a few more spaces for the first line of a paragraph) and single space if you are typing. The following example is from a student research paper.

QUOTATION MARKS

The author sums up in a nutshell the basic conditions that have shaped Spain's cultural development:

> Spain is a world apart from the rest of Europe, separated by climatic differences and isolated in time as well as in space. Bounded by water on three sides, and on the fourth cut off by the barrier of the Pyrenees, she was for three hundred years, from the VIIIth to the XIth centuries, virtually under the domination of a Muslim power, that of the Moors, whose culture was not only more advanced than that of any part of Europe, but also profoundly different from any European civilization.
>
> —Enriqueta Harris, *Spanish Painting*

When quoting one or two lines of poetry, follow the example for a directly quoted passage:

- W. H. Auden refers to European politics before World War Two when he says, "In the nightmare of the dark / All the dogs of Europe bark...." [Note the slash to show the end of the line.]

When quoting more than two lines of poetry, do not use quotation marks. Simply indent the whole passage as for long prose quotations, single space if typing, and reproduce the original as it stands.

2. *Use quotation marks to emphasize words used in an unusual sense:*

- In the printing trade, an engraved plate is called a "cut."

NOTE: Do not use quotation marks to ask acceptance for lazy, imprecise language of your own.

> **MISUSE:** In spite of Nicola's "goofing off," she was generally regarded as a very "sharp" character.

3. *Use quotation marks to set off the titles of chapters of a book; episodes of a TV or radio series; and the titles of*

articles, short stories, and poems published as part of a complete book, magazine, or newspaper:

- One of my favourite short stories is D. H. Lawrence's "A Rocking Horse Winner."

The title of the whole book is underlined, or italicized, whereas the chapter title is in quotation marks:

- When you read *Sister Carrie*, pay careful attention to the first chapter, "The Magnet Attracting: A Waif Amid Forces."

The series title of a TV or radio show is underlined, whereas the title of an individual episode is in quotation marks:

- Last week I watched an excellent program called "The Winged World" on *Best of the National Geographic Specials*.

NOTE: Do not use quotation marks around the title of your own essay or other writing. Do not underline your own title. To set it off clearly from the beginning of your essay, just skip a line or two between your title and your first paragraph.

HOW TO USE QUOTATION MARKS WITH OTHER PUNCTUATION

1. *Place periods, commas, and other punctuation marks inside closing quotation marks:*

- Shakespeare said, "Out, out, brief candle!"

- E. M. Forster, in commenting on the value of a human being, said, "Man is the measure.... Man's feet are the measure for distance, his hands are the measure for ownership, his body is the measure for all that is loveable and desirable and strong."

2. *Place colons and semicolons outside closing quotation marks:*

- We arrive at "the moment of truth": the matador extends his sword for the final thrust.

- I know that "to err is human"; yet fifteen errors in one ball game is too much to forgive.

3. *Place question marks and exclamation points inside closing quotation marks only if they are a part of the quoted passage:*

- He asked him, "Is dinner ready?"

- She shouted, "Score the goal!"

Place question marks and exclamation points outside the quotation marks if they are *not* part of the quoted passage:

- Did I just hear you say, "Dinner is ready"?

- Stop saying "yes"!

In direct quotations, avoid the unnecessary comma or period with a closing quotation mark:

> **AVOID:** "Well, well!", he said. [Remove the comma.]
> **AVOID:** "Well, well!," he said. [Remove the comma.]
> **BETTER:** "Well, well!" he said.

> **AVOID:** He asked, "What's your name?". [Remove the period.]
> **BETTER:** He asked, "What's your name?"

4. *Use single quotation marks (' ') to set off a quotation within a quotation:*

- "When Caesar said 'I came, I saw, I conquered,'" my history teacher declared, "little did he know that he had invented the telegram."

If you quote an essay title that quotes another title, use single quotation marks for the quoted title within the title:

• I just read a journal article about Robert Frost and his poem "Two Tramps in Mud Time." The title of the article is "Frost and the Work Ethic: 'Two Tramps in Mud Time.'"

In the journal, the title has no quotation marks around it, but the title of the poem it quotes is set in *double* quotation marks:

• Frost and the Work Ethic: "Two Tramps in Mud Time."

REPETITION ———————— rep

Do not unnecessarily repeat the same word or idea you have used before. (See *Wordiness*.)

The more serious problem is the repetition of the same idea—whether in similar form or not—throughout the whole length of a composition. (See **Paragraph**.) Such repetition suggests that you have little to say but feel pressured to fill up space. The following examples show awkward uses of repetition and correction of the awkwardness:

REPETITION: A cool breeze was *blowing*, and the brownish gold leaves were being *blown* about by the wind.

Change *blown* to *scattered*, or find another good synonym. Sometimes, as in this case, the sentence would be better if it were condensed. There is no need to refer to the breeze again, even by the synonym *wind*:

REVISION: The brownish gold leaves were being scattered by the cool breeze.

REPETITION: The air was too cold, *and* while I was asleep it chilled me, *and* when I awoke my bones felt stiff. [Eliminate one of the *and's*.]

REVISION: The air was too cold. While I was asleep it chilled me, and when I awoke my bones felt stiff.

REPETITION: I want to earn a college diploma because I would like many options to remain open to me in the future because rapid technological changes leave people without post-secondary education at a great disadvantage. [Avoid the *because... because* construction.]
REVISION: I want to earn a college diploma because I would like many options to remain open to me in the future. Rapid technological changes leave people without post-secondary education at a great disadvantage.

REPETITION: The steam could be seen rising from the radiator. *The steam* turned to frost on the windowpane. [Delete the second *steam* and combine the two sentences.]
REVISION: The steam rising from the radiator turned to frost on the windowpane.

REPETITION: He kept changing his mind *and failed to stick with a single idea he came up with*.
REVISION: He kept changing his mind. [Avoid needlessly repeating an idea.]

Repetition is not always bad (See **Parallelism**). Repetition of words or ideas can be used deliberately to arouse emotion or aid memory. We find such conscious repetition in the most varied kinds of communication, from commercial advertising and political propaganda to poetry and oratory. The last major speech of Martin Luther King, Jr. is unforgettable because of the mounting repetitions, "I have a dream..." And in the Bible, Ecclesiastes 3:1-3, the repetitions sound with a poetic beat: "To every thing there is a season, and a time to every purpose under the heaven. A time to be born, and a time to die; a time to plant, and a time to pluck up that which is planted; a time to kill, and a time to heal..."

RUN-ON SENTENCE ——— run

Do not run one sentence into the next. Separate them with proper punctuation or a coordinating conjunction.

End the first sentence with a period or other end-of-sentence punctuation such as a question mark or exclamation point and begin the next sentence with a capital letter. A semicolon will sometimes work better than a period or conjunction. (See **Semicolon,** 2.) In any case, do not join two sentences with only a comma. Although this comma error is sometimes called a run-on sentence, it is usually referred to as a comma splice (See **Comma Splice.**):

> **RUN-ON:** Virtual Reality is a life-like three-dimensional computer world it inhabits what is called "cyberspace."
> **REVISION:** Virtual Reality is a life-like three-dimensional computer world. It inhabits what is called "cyberspace."

> **RUN-ON:** She put on her bathing cap then she plunged into the water.
> **REVISION 1:** She put on her bathing cap. Then she plunged into the water.

Although a period is correct, a semicolon would probably be better between *cap* and *then*. (Look up the use of semicolons before conjunctive adverbs like *then*, *however*, and *therefore* under **Comma Splice.**)

> **REVISION 2:** She put on her bathing cap, then plunged into the water.

Use fewer words wherever convenient. By eliminating the second *she* and adding a comma after *cap*, you are left with a single, smooth sentence.

SEMICOLON

RUN-ON: The snow fell all night in the morning the air was crystal clear.
REVISION I: The snow fell all night. In the morning the air was crystal clear.
REVISION 2: The snow fell all night, but in the morning the air was crystal clear.

Sometimes a comma and a coordinating conjunction such as *but* or *and* make a smoother sentence. (See **Comma,** 1.)

NOTE: When sentences are short, they may be joined with a coordinating conjunction and no punctuation:

• He ran *and* she hid.

semi ;/ ─────── SEMICOLON

1. Use the semicolon to connect two main clauses when they are closely related in idea.
2. Use the semicolon to separate sentence elements equal in rank when they contain commas.

I. CONNECTING MAIN (INDEPENDENT) CLAUSES

Use the semicolon to connect two related complete sentences, generally when they are not connected with a coordinating conjunction such as *and, but, for, or, nor* :

• It is not so much the threatening weather that concerns me; it is the rusting condition of the ship. [The ideas are closely related.]

Also use the semicolon between main clauses connected by certain conjunctive adverbs, such as *however, therefore, then, similarly, likewise.* (See **Comma Splice.**)

• The written part of the exam does not bother Carlene; however, to become a police officer she should also be able to bench-press at least half her weight.

Do not use the semicolon between a main clause and a phrase or subordinate clause:

AVOID: I do not like to eat orange peels; although I admit that in marmalade they are quite good. [Remove the semicolon.]
BETTER: I do not like to eat orange peels although I admit that in marmalade they are quite good. [No punctuation is normally needed between a main and a subordinate clause.] [See **Subordination** for a list of *subordinating conjunctions* that will help you to identify subordinate clauses.]

2. SEPARATING EQUAL ELEMENTS

Use the semicolon to show the main divisions in equal sentence elements containing commas:

• I introduced him to Alicia Soto, the president; Larry Wilson, the vice-president; and Asgar Amani, the treasurer.

-S ERROR IN -S ENDINGS ———— -s error

Add an "s"-ending to your verb or omit an "s" ending from your verb.

Standard English contradicts the speech habits of many people when it comes to the endings of verbs in the present tense. Remember that the noun and verb must agree [see **Agreement**].

-S ERROR IN -S ENDINGS

NONSTANDARD: He *like* to play baseball. [The "s" is missing from *likes*.]
STANDARD: He *likes* to play baseball.

NONSTANDARD: My cousin *work* all night and *sleep* all day.
STANDARD: My cousin *works* all night and *sleeps* all day.

NONSTANDARD: I *limits* myself to two hours of TV a day. [The "s" should be omitted from *limits*.]
STANDARD: I *limit* myself to two hours of TV a day.

NONSTANDARD: They just never *stops* talking.
STANDARD: They just never *stop* talking.

NONSTANDARD: Today's women *appreciates* the importance of a good education.
STANDARD: Today's women *appreciate* the importance of a good education.

When do you keep the "s" and when do you omit it? The pattern is simple:

• Present-tense verbs following the pronouns *he*, *she*, and *it* end in "s." (He goes; she drives; it smells.)

• Present-tense verbs following the pronouns *I, you, we,* and *they* do not end in "s." (I go; you drive; we try; they smell.)

• In the same way, present-tense verbs following nouns that substitute for *he, she,* and *it* end in "s": John (instead of *he*) goes; Ella (for *she*) drives; the barn (for *it*) smells. Also, present-tense verbs following nouns that substitute for *we* and *they* do not end in "s": Nguyen and I (instead of *we*) work hard; apples (for *they*) taste good.

NOTE: For a more detailed grammatical explanation of this pattern, see **Agreement,** 1.

SEXIST EXPRESSION ——— sex

Avoid terms that refer to only one gender if they unfairly exclude the other. Whenever possible, use plural pronouns or occupational titles that reflect equal treatment of the sexes.

I. SEXIST PRONOUNS

A special problem in the use of pronouns may occur when the following words are used as antecedents: *each, every, everyone, everybody, everything, someone, somebody, anyone, anybody, no one, nobody, either, neither, another.* Although they may occur in a sentence as antecedents, these words are themselves singular pronouns and should be referred to by singular pronouns. This opens the possibility of sexist language.

> **EXAMPLE:** *Each of us* knows *his* job. [While *us* refers to a group—and so is plural—*each* changes this to a collection of singular individuals. The use of *his* assumes that each of us consists entirely of males.]
> **EXAMPLE:** *Each* of the women presented *her* opinion.

NOTE: When any of these antecedents stands for a group of both men and women, you have several options:

A. You may use a double pronoun: Each of us knows *his* or *her* job well. Because double references can get cumbersome if overused, try the following alternate ways to represent both males and females in a group.

B. Leave out the pronouns entirely where possible:

> **CORRECT:** Everyone made *his* or *her* presentation.
> **BETTER:** Everyone made a presentation.

C. Use plurals where possible:

> **CORRECT:** Everyone made *his* or *her* presentation.
> **BETTER:** *All managers* made *their* presentations.

D. When omitting the pronouns or using the plural is not possible, write or rewrite to avoid implying that the group you are referring to, which actually includes both men and women, is composed exclusively of men:

> **MISLEADING:** Anyone, if *he* works hard enough, can succeed.
> **BETTER:** Anyone *who* works hard enough can succeed.

E. In passages requiring repeated use of a pronoun referring to someone *in general*, not to a specific person of known sex, it has become accepted practice to use *feminine* pronouns throughout at least the first such passage. (You may continue to do so throughout your essay, or you may prefer to *alternate* passages that use feminine pronouns with those using exclusively masculine pronouns—provided you do not confuse the reader.)

> **EXAMPLE:** (passage not about a specific individual): The writer who wishes to succeed in her chosen field needs more than just talent. She needs enormous self-confidence and the ability to take a stream of rejection slips in stride. Beyond that, she needs perseverance—maintenance of a rigorous work schedule and patience to wait years for recognition.

NOTE: If you remember to use *plurals* wherever possible (see C above), you can avoid choosing a gender-specific pronoun altogether and write the above paragraph as follows:

Writers who wish to succeed in *their* chosen field need more than just talent. *They* need enormous self-confidence and the ability to take a stream of rejection slips in stride. Beyond that, *they* need perseverance—maintenance of a rigorous work schedule and patience to wait years for recognition.

2. SEXIST OCCUPATIONAL TITLES

Avoid labeling an occupation as belonging particularly to one gender. If you use the word *foreman*, for instance, you may suggest to your readers—even without meaning to—that you assume anyone in charge of a work crew to be a male. Although such language is in common use, many people consider it sexist, implying prejudice against one of the sexes. Instead of *foreman* you might use a gender-neutral term like *supervisor* or *section head*. Some common sexist expressions and their nondiscriminatory alternatives follow:

Sexist	Alternative
Businessman	Business executive, business owner, business person, company head, manufacturer, wholesaler
Chairman	Chair, chairperson
Fireman	Firefighter
Foreman	Supervisor
Garbageman	Sanitation worker
Housewife	Housekeeper, domestic engineer
Mailman/postman	Postal clerk, letter carrier
Manpower	Workers, workforce, personnel
Marksman	Sharpshooter
Policeman	Police officer
Repairman	Service technician
Salesman/saleswoman	Sales clerk, salesperson, sales representative
Weatherman	Meteorologist, weather forecaster
Workman	Worker, labourer, employee

slang ─────────────── SLANG

Avoid the use of slang—catchy, colourful words or phrases currently in use by seemingly everyone, especially the media—when writing formal English.

Slang expressions tend to be popular for a few years but soon sound dated and are replaced by other, equally glittery statements. Many years ago people used to say "copasetic"—a word recognized only by specialists today—to express the same kind of approval as is now generally rendered by "awesome." Some slang expressions, however, do not die out but enrich the language permanently as *colloquialisms* or *clichés*. While the use of these in informal writing can be acceptable, they still sound largely out of place in formal written English. The problem for any writer is how to sound fresh and interesting without using slang or any other kind of overused language. (See hints for improving your style under **Triteness** and **Diction**.)

MISUSE OF SLANG IN A FORMAL CONTEXT: The High Commissioner decided to *deep six* his appointment with the British Prime Minister when the Scotland Yard *dudes* warned of a terrorist attack. Our *rep* can be such a *bozo,* though, when explaining himself in public, that it sounded as if he did not care *diddly-squat* about his British counterpart. His problem is that he is *uptight* in front of the cameras and never quite learned how to *cool out*.

REWRITTEN VERSION OF THE ABOVE: The High Commissioner decided to cancel his appointment with the British Prime Minister when the Scotland Yard police warned of a terrorist attack. Our national representative can be so awkward, though, when explaining himself in public, that it sounded as if he did not have much respect for his British counterpart. His problem is that he is nervous in front of the cameras and never quite learned how to relax.

SLASH ———————————— slash /

Use the slash in certain instances to separate specific kinds of English expressions.

The slash is used to separate items of information such as elements of an abbreviated date, alternative words, lines of poetry, and parts of fractions.

> **EXAMPLE:** The memo was dated 12/5/97. [Elements of a date]
> **EXAMPLE:** The grading in this subject is pass/fail. [Alternative words]
> **EXAMPLE:** In "Stopping by Woods on a Snowy Evening," Robert Frost wrote, "For I have promises to keep / And miles to go before I sleep." [Separating lines of quoted poetry. Notice the space before and after the slash.]
> **EXAMPLE:** Use a 3/8 inch drill-bit. [Separating the elements of a fraction]

> **OVERUSE OF SLASH:** Avoid the telegraphic style that results from the use of the slash [/] to connect closely related items by writers too impatient to express their ideas in a clear, logical sequence.

> **ABUSE OF SLASH:** Our present administrative policy/program is now bankrupt.

SPLIT INFINITIVE ————— split

Do not split infinitives unnecessarily.

To speak, to go, to think are infinitives. You split the infinitive *to speak* when you place a word or words between *to* and *speak*: *to hastily speak* or *to now and then speak*. In formal writing, split infinitives are now acceptable if they read

97

smoothly. Sometimes it is less awkward to split an infinitive than not to split it, but that is not often the case:

UNACCEPTABLE: He foolishly tried *to*, without studying at all, *pass* the marketing final.
REVISED: He foolishly tried *to pass* the marketing final without studying at all.

UNACCEPTABLE: He manages *to* usually *bore* people to death.
REVISED: He usually manages *to bore* people to death.

ACCEPTABLE: He managed *to* completely *undermine* the work of the committee. [If you try to place *completely* elsewhere—before *to*, after *undermine*, or after *committee*—the sentence will not read as smoothly as it does with the split infinitive.]

sub —————— SUBORDINATION

Emphasize important ideas by keeping them as main clauses. Change lesser ideas into subordinate clauses, phrases, and even single words where possible. (See *Variety in Sentence Patterns*.)

COORDINATE SENTENCE STRUCTURE

In sentence structure, *subordination* is the opposite of *coordination*. *Coordination* is the use of word groups that are structurally equal to express ideas that are equal in importance. Julius Caesar's "I came, I saw, I conquered" is a good example of main clauses arranged in a coordinate series.

More typically, coordinate structures are joined by any of the following words, which are called coordinating conjunctions: *and, but, or, nor, for, yet, so.* For example, "I jog *and* I swim, *but* I do not play tennis."

SUBORDINATE SENTENCE STRUCTURE

Subordination is the use of word groups that are structurally unequal to express ideas that are unequal in importance: "I read the book because I liked the movie." Here the main idea is in the main clause, *I read the book*, and the less important, or subordinate, idea is in the subordinate clause, *because I liked the movie*. The main clause, containing the main idea, can stand alone as a sentence: *I read the book*; but the subordinate clause, containing the less important idea, cannot stand by itself.

Subordinate clauses begin with subordinating conjunctions or relative pronouns. ["Subordinate clause" is defined under **Variety in Sentence Patterns**.] Here is a list of common subordinators:

Subordinating Conjunctions

after	because	provided	whenever
although	before	since	where
as	even though	so that	wherever
as if	if	though	while
as long as	in order that	unless	why
as soon as	no matter how	until	
as though	once	when	

Relative Pronouns

that	which	whoever	whomever
what	who	whom	whose

STRINGY SENTENCES: Do not use coordination—stringing ideas together with *and* or *so*—when subordination would better express the relationship of the ideas.

STRINGY: I saw the movie three times *and* I always found it more fascinating each time, *so* I finally read the book.

BETTER: I finally read the book *because, after seeing* the movie three times, I realized I always found it more fascinating each time.

CHOPPY SENTENCES

Another form of abusing coordination is writing a series of short, choppy sentences even though the ideas are *not* of equal importance:

CHOPPY: People were bored. We became irritable. The picnic broke up early.

If you use *subordination*, however, you can show more clearly how these ideas are connected and express them in one smooth sentence:

BETTER: *Becoming irritable out of sheer boredom,* we broke up our picnic early.

(See **Choppy Sentences.**)

Further examples of sentences requiring the use of subordination follow:

STRINGY: Hossein's employer did not care for him, *so* she refused to write him a letter of recommendation. [Two equally emphatic main clauses.]

BETTER: *Because* Hossein's employer did not care for him, she refused to write him a letter of recommendation.

[The first main clause, less emphatic than the second, is changed into a subordinate clause beginning with *because*.]

CHOPPY: She was exhausted. She had been swimming too long and was doubled up by a sudden cramp. She shouted for help. [This is an awkward series of choppy sentences.]
BETTER: Exhausted from swimming too long *and* doubled up by a sudden cramp, she shouted for help. [The first two sentences are turned into phrases.]

STRINGY: The moon *was glowing, and it* looked like the face of a snowman.
BETTER: The *glowing* moon looked like the face of a snowman. [The first main clause is condensed into the single word *glowing*.]

TENSE _____ tense, t/

1. **Check to see whether you are using the proper sequence of tenses. One of the verbs in your sentence may not be in the correct time relation with the other(s).**
2. **Use your dictionary to find the correct forms of irregular verbs (for example, choose, chose, chosen).**
3. **Do not shift tenses without good reason. (See Point of View, 2.)**
4. **Use the present tense to present plot summaries and your statements of an author's ideas.**

Tense is the form of a verb that tells your reader the *time*— past, present, or future—in which the action takes place. The

TENSE

verb *form* is the clue to the time. Here are three tense forms of the verb *to work*: present (I *work*, he *works*); past (he *worked*); future (he *will work*).

I. SEQUENCE OF TENSES

If the time when an action takes place is the *same* in both the main clause and the subordinate clause, then the tense of both verbs must be the same:

• When she *arrived*, the crowd *greeted* her with a long ovation.

• As he slowly *turns*, he *balances* himself with his arms.

If the action in the subordinate clause takes place before that in the main clause, put the subordinate verb in the appropriate past tense:

• I *hear* that he *has worked* wonders.

The main verb, *hear*, is in the present tense; the subordinate verb, *has worked*, is in the present perfect tense. The present perfect tense expresses a time earlier than the present.

• I *heard* that he *had worked* wonders.

The past perfect, *had worked*, expresses a time prior to some understood time in the past. This *understood* past time is expressed by the simple past tense, *heard*.

When you are expressing a permanent fact, always use the present tense:

• I learned that the moon always *presents* the same face to the Earth. [Use *presents*, not *presented*.]

Keep an infinitive in the present tense if it expresses the same time as the action of the main verb; keep it in the past tense if it expresses a time before the action of the main verb:

• I would have liked *to go* with you.

• I would like *to go* with you.

In both these cases, although the main verb differs in tense, the present infinitive concerns *going* at the same time that the liking or the desire to go is expressed.

• I would like *to have gone* with you.

Here the past infinitive is used because the wish in the present concerns an action already completed in the past.

OVERKILL: I would *have liked to have gone* with you.

Do not use the past infinitive together with the past tense of the main verb. Use one or the other, as shown in the earlier examples, but not both at the same time.

2. IRREGULAR VERBS

Most English verbs are *regular*, forming their past tense and past participle with *-ed*: I *waited*, I have *waited*. With a regular verb like *wait*, once you know the present tense, you know all the other tenses.

There is a troublesome group of *irregular verbs*, however, whose present tense (I *break*) is no clue to the past tense (I *broke*) or to the compound past tenses formed with the past participle (I *have broken*: *broken* is the past participle).

If you are in doubt about the past tense forms of a verb, look up the verb in the dictionary under its present-tense form (*bite*, for example) and you will find the past tense (*bit*) and past participle (*bitten*) listed in order right after it. Here is a list of some of the most frequently misused irregular verbs:

TENSE

Present	Past	Past Participle
I *blow*	I *blew*	I have *blown*
I *bring*	I *brought*	I have *brought*
I *burst*	I *burst*	I have *burst*
I *do*	I *did*	I have *done*
I *drink*	I *drank*	I have *drunk*
I *drive*	I *drove*	I have *driven*
I *eat*	I *ate*	I have *eaten*
I *forbid*	I *forbade*	I have *forbidden*
I *go*	I *went*	I have *gone*
I *lay* (bricks)	I *laid* (bricks)	I have *laid* (bricks)
I *lie* (down)	I *lay* (down)	I have *lain* (down)
I *ring*	I *rang*	I have *rung*
I *rise*	I *rose*	I have *risen*
I *run*	I *ran*	I have *run*
I *seek*	I *sought*	I have *sought*
I *sing*	I *sang*	I have *sung*
I *steal*	I *stole*	I have *stolen*
I *swim*	I *swam*	I have *swum*
I *swing*	I *swung*	I have *swung*
I *write*	I *wrote*	I have *written*

3. TENSE SHIFTS

Changes in tense must occur for a good reason. In the following example, there is no justification for the shift:

> **SHIFT:** I *ran* to his house and *tried* to find him, but I *arrive* too late.
> **REVISED:** I ran to his house and tried to find him, but I *arrived* too late.

If it seems natural to you to use *arrive* rather than *arrived*, it may be that in your daily speech habits you are not used to using, or even hearing, the past-tense endings of verbs in standard English. If this is so, ask your instructor to recommend materials that will help you practise the standard tense forms. (See also **-Ed Error in -Ed Endings**.)

4. PRESENT TENSE IN PLOT SUMMARIES

It does not matter whether the origial story was written in the past tense, or whether the author whose ideas you are reporting is long dead. Always use the *present tense* under the following circumstances:

For plot summaries: In Part IV of Jonathan Swift's *Gulliver's Travels*, Gulliver *becomes* the guest of a race of highly civilized horses who *are* the masters of a slave-race of degenerate Yahoos. Gulliver *discovers* to his horror, the physically and morally disgusting Yahoos *are* very similar to human beings.

For your statement of an author's ideas: In *Gulliver's Travels*, Swift *weighs* man against beast and *concludes* that so-called "civilized" man *is* a moral monster who *ranks* far below any beast.

THESIS ———————————— thes

Clarify the thesis statement of your essay.

In an extended essay, the thesis, or preview statement, states your main idea and your approach to it. It includes both your subject and your main point about the subject. In essence, a thesis statement acts like a road map for your whole essay, informing your reader of where you are going and how you will get there.

There are three questions that you should ask yourself as you develop your thesis statement. These are the following:

1. What is my general topic?
2. What is my limited subject?
3. What point do I want to make?

Here are some examples:

General Topic	Limited Subject	Point
Problems of transportation	Problems with too many cars Cars contribute to air pollution	
Education	Choosing subjects Courses in a post-secondary program that lead to a marketing diploma Certain career choices enhance employment options	
Habits	Breaking bad habits Quitting smoking Making a behaviour change involves great will-power	

In each of these cases, you narrow your general topic down to a limited subject and decide exactly what you want to say about it. From the point, or thesis, the audience, or reader, builds an expectation about what you are going to discuss in your essay.

Problems In Writing A Thesis Statement

TOO BROAD: If you are to write a three hundred word essay and your thesis statement is "A long history has led to the crisis of French and English in Canada," you will not be able to handle your thesis within the specified length. You must narrow your thesis statement to something that can be handled within the scope of your assignment.

TOO NARROW: "Generation X followed the baby-boomers." This is a statement of fact and gives you little to discuss, especially within the requirement of three hundred words.

TOO VAGUE: "Unemployment is a major problem that society must address." This does not tell your reader anything about the point that you want to make. Will you discuss the causes of unemployment or suggest solutions?

ANNOUNCEMENTS: "In this essay, I will discuss the effect of climate on crop production." This does not tell your reader anything that they do not already know. What direction will your essay take?

TOPIC SENTENCE ——— top

Revise your topic statement so that it makes a clear point.

A topic sentence states the main point of a paragraph. All other sentences within the paragraph relate directly to the topic sentence.

Just as the thesis statement provides a focus for the whole essay, the topic sentence provides a focus for the paragraph. [See **Thesis**.]

Problems In Writing Topic Sentences

TOO BROAD: "Gardening is an activity enjoyed by many Canadians." The scope of this statement is too great to be handled in a single paragraph.

TOO NARROW: "I plant tomatoes in my garden." After this statement, there is little that can follow it.

ANNOUNCEMENTS: "This paragraph is about gardening." Clearly, if the paragraph is about gardening, your reader will realize this as they read.

GOOD: "Gardening in southern British Columbia requires a careful selection of plants."

trans ——————— TRANSITIONS

Use a word or phrase to form a logical bridge, or *transition*, between two thoughts. The best transition to use is the one that most exactly expresses the logical relationship between two thoughts, sentences, or paragraphs.

Transitions are a special group of words and phrases that show how a piece of writing progresses logically from one idea to the next. Transitions connect parts of sentences, one sentence to another, and one paragraph to another. They express logical relations between ideas such as addition (*also, besides, furthermore*), contrast (*but, however, on the contrary*), result (*therefore, consequently*), and space or time (*beyond, in the distance, now, afterwards*). The following passage uses transitions of time (in italics):

> In its earliest stages, war consisted solely of battle for hunting grounds. *Afterwards*, war involved struggles for pasture. *Later*, war was fought for tilled or tillable land.

There are many ways of showing the logical linkage between ideas. Commonly used transitions follow:

Transitional Words

accordingly	eventually	later	second
actually	finally	likewise	similarly
afterward	first	meanwhile	soon
again	further	moreover	still
also	furthermore	nevertheless	then
and	gradually	next	therefore
before	hence	nonetheless	thereupon
beforehand	here	notwithstanding	this
besides	however	nor	too
but	indeed	now	
consequently	last	otherwise	

Transitional Phrases

after all	for instance	in spite of (that)
all in all	for this purpose	in sum
all things consid-	generally speaking	in the first place
ered	in addition	in the meantime
and yet	in any event	in the past
as a result	in brief	on the contrary
at length	in contrast	on the other hand
at the same time	in fact	on the whole
by the same token	in like manner	to be sure
for example	in other words	to sum up
for the most part	in short	to this end

WEAK TRANSITION: She lost one fortune *and*, as if to spite fate, rapidly accumulated a second.
BETTER: She lost one fortune *but*, as if to spite fate, rapidly accumulated a second. [*But* more forcefully expresses the intended contrast.]

TRANSITION MISSING: I liked him. I thought his table manners needed improving. [The sudden contrast between these two thoughts is not smoothly bridged.]
BETTER: I liked him; *however*, I thought his table manners needed improving.

TRANSITION MISSING: On the whole, I think that educated people have made the best politicians. There are exceptions. [The second sentence follows too abruptly.]
BETTER: On the whole, I think that educated people have made the best politicians. *Of course*, there are exceptions.

Note the use of transitional words and phrases (italicized) in the following paragraph:

During the spring, I intend to get back into shape. *At first*, I will begin by jogging a kilometre per day. *As my stamina builds*, I will extend this to five kilometres per day. I *also* plan to begin weight training to build my strength. *By the fall*, I will be playing football *and*, in winter I will play hockey.

(For further information see **Coherence; Logic,** 5; and **Paragraph.**)

trite ——————————— TRITENESS

Rewrite the marked passage to eliminate the triteness.

Trite writing is dull, commonplace, and uninteresting. The fault may lie in the thought or the phrasing—and frequently in both. Use the following suggestions to eliminate triteness from your writing:

1. *Use livelier verbs.* Many common verbs do not make for specific, lively writing. Instead of writing, "I *had to eat* my sandwich quickly," write, "I *wolfed down* my sandwich."

   Which is more effective, "The elderly patient *walked slowly* down the hospital corridor," or "The elderly patient *shuffled* down the hospital corridor"?

2. *Use precise, vivid adjectives.* Many adjectives—*handsome, beautiful, nice, ugly*—are too vague to create a clear, specific picture in the reader's mind. You should communicate as precisely as possible the specific picture you have in mind. Instead of writing, "My father has a *handsome face* and *nice eyes*," write something like, "My father has a *weather-beaten sportsman's face* with *gentle brown eyes*."

3. *Use effective figures of speech (comparisons).* Sometimes comparing one thing to another does the job better than a written explanation containing many words. Instead of writing, "We tried to get him to confess, *but he would not tell us a thing*," write, "We tried to get him to confess, but he was *as silent as a rock*."

CLICHÉS

A comparison that grows out of the situation you are writing about is likely to be fresh and appealing. A figure of speech that you have heard before is likely to be a cliché. Clichés are a special case of triteness. They are expressions that were once vivid and picturesque but are now so commonly used that they have lost their original force. Here are some examples of clichés (italicized):

- I got up *on the wrong side of the bed* this morning.
- He wanted to live out in *the wide open spaces.*
- They made progress *by leaps and bounds.*
- On picnics one can relax and enjoy *Mother Nature.*
- I felt *as cool as a cucumber.*
- No one suspected the *trials and tribulations* they went through.
- Her cousin was *as quiet as a mouse.*
- Nicola tried *really* hard.

VAGUENESS ——————— vague

Rewrite the marked section in clear, direct, precise language.

Vague writing is often described as *foggy* or *cloudy* because it lacks substance. It relies heavily on generalization and lacks specific, concrete ideas and facts. (See **Abstract Expressions**; **Diction**; and **Logic**, 2.)

There is nothing wrong with a clear, substantial generalization; for example, "Students who do not read well are unable to write well." You may not agree with this statement, but at least you have something specific to discuss. Compare that statement with this: "Students with problems in some areas have other problems as well." This statement is fuzzy, insubstantial, and evasive. It does not challenge the reader to think about a clear issue. It makes a noise without making a point.

Vague writing is like a picture out of focus. To develop a clear, precise writing style, focus your mind on the idea or image you want to present before you commit it to paper. If you see it clearly in your mind, you have a good chance of bringing it out clearly on paper. Foggy writing mirrors foggy thinking:

> **VAGUE:** Professor Chan is a tough teacher whose personality turns me off.
> **CLEARER:** Professor Chan grades much too harshly and is insulting to students who challenge her ideas.

> **VAGUE:** I voted again for Mayor Ayala because her policies have helped the city improve in many ways, as we can see all around us.
> **CLEARER:** I voted again for Mayor Ayala because she has erased the city's budget deficit, built a new hospital and library, and helped improve relations between the police and the public.

VARIETY IN
var ——— SENTENCE PATTERNS

Develop a lively style by varying the structures and lengths of your sentences.

Good writers are always juggling a limited number of basic sentence patterns, balancing one against another to avoid monotony and to create a pleasing, rhythmic flow. You will find these basic structures easy to remember *because you know them already*; you already possess an array of skills that you are probably not aware that you have. Substituting one pattern for another, we shall run a sample passage through a sequence of changes to show how virtually the same ideas can be expressed through a variety *of forms*.

I. STRUCTURAL VARIETY

Simple, Compound, and Complex Sentences

SAMPLE PASSAGE: We lost the first game. We vowed to even the score the next day. [Here we have two *simple sentences*. Each simple sentence contains only one subject verb nucleus—"We lost," "we vowed." The sentences stand uninterestingly next to each other. Notice how in the following examples the use of certain standard word structures creates meaningful relationships between these now separate ideas.]

USING COORDINATION: We lost the first game, *but* we vowed to even the score the next day. [We now have a *compound sentence*, which is at least two simple sentences connected by a coordinating conjunction—*and, but, or, nor, for, yet*, or *so*. The connection by *but* ties these two separate thoughts into a relationship of contrast.]

USING A SUBORDINATE CLAUSE: *After we lost the first game*, we vowed to even the score the next day. [A *subordinate clause* consists of a subordinating conjunction—like *after, because, since, when, although*—followed by, at the least, a subject and its verb—*we lost*. Try substituting *although* for *after*.]

USING A RELATIVE CLAUSE: After we lost the first game, we vowed *that we would even the score the next day* [A *relative clause* is a type of subordinate clause normally beginning with a relative pronoun such as *that, what, which, who*, or *whom*. Note: The combination of a main clause (simple sentence) with a subordinate clause results in a *complex sentence*. One of the ways to gain variety in sentence patterns is to create a pleasing alternation of *simple, compound*, and *complex* sentences.]

The following paragraph, from an essay by Robert Jay Lifton in *The Final Epidemic*, illustrates the skillful alternation of simple, compound, and complex sentences:

> Although the idea of apocalypse has been with us throughout the ages, it has been within a religious context—the idea that God will punish and even eliminate man for his sins. [*complex*] Now it is our own technology and we are doing it ourselves. [*compound*] Nor is it only the nuclear threat. [*simple*] There are chemical warfare and germ warfare; destruction of the environment, the air we breathe or the ozone layer; and depletion of the world's resources, whether of energy or food. [*simple*]

Different Types of Phrases

SAMPLE PASSAGE: We lost the first game. We vowed to even the score the next day.

USING A PARTICIPIAL PHRASE: *Having lost the first game*, we vowed to even the score the next day. [A *participial phrase* is a group of words beginning with a participle, the *-ing* form of a verb: in our example, *having*. It acts as an adjective and modifies the subject, *we*, of the main clause it introduces.]

USING A GERUND PHRASE: *Losing the first game* made us vow to even the score the next day. [A *gerund phrase* looks like a participial phrase. It starts with a gerund, also the *-ing* form of a verb: in our example, *losing*. A gerund or whole gerund phrase acts as a noun. Here it acts as the subject of a sentence whose verb is *made*.]

USING A PREPOSITIONAL PHRASE: *After that first-game defeat*, we vowed to even the score the next day. [A *prepositional phrase*, like *before work, inside the CBC,* or *after our defeat,* consists of a preposition followed by a noun—*defeat*—and any modifiers of that noun—*that first-game*.]

Here is a list of some common prepositions:

about	beside	from	on	until
above	between	in	over	up
after	but	into	since	with
around	by	like	through	within
at	during	near	to	without
before	except	of	toward	
below	for	off	under	

> **USING AN INFINITIVE PHRASE:** *To have lost the first game* was such a blow that we vowed to even the score the next day. [An *infinitive phrase* starts with an infinitive—in our example, *to have lost*—which is followed by a noun, *game*, and any modifiers of that noun, *the first*. The infinitive phrase in this example acts as one whole noun, the subject of a sentence whose verb is *was*. Note that this sentence is also *complex*, consisting of a main clause beginning with *To have lost* and a subordinate clause beginning with *that*.]

For more information on sentence patterns, see **Subordination**. To learn how to knit sentences together to form a smooth paragraph, see **Transitions** and **Paragraph**.

Here is a brief paragraph, modified from J. E. Oliver's *Perspectives on Applied Physical Geography*, that achieves sentence variety by using subordination, coordination, and all of the phrase types we have discussed:

> *Making use of loud noises* [gerund phrase] has been tried all over the world as a means *to change the weather.* [infinitive phrase] *In Europe, for example,* [prepositional phrases] people have tried *to prevent hailstorms,* [infinitive phrase] *for* [coordinating conjunction] hail has always caused considerable damage to vineyards. *To stop the hail from forming* [infinitive phrase] farmers in northern Italy fired cannons at thunderclouds. Others felt *that they could stop storms* [relative clause] *by ringing* church bells loudly. [gerund phrase] Surprisingly, in some places *ringing bells and firing cannons* [gerund phrases] did seem to reduce the amount of crop damage

by hail. This method became so popular *that it was finally outlawed.* [relative clause] Too many people were killed *by misfiring cannons* [prepositional phrase] and *by lightning* [prepositional phrase] *striking bell towers* [participial phrase].

2. SENTENCE-LENGTH VARIETY

Good writers vary the pace and rhythm of their prose by mixing long, short, and medium-length sentences in any extended passage, as in the following paragraph (slightly modified from *Lunar Science: A Post-Apollo View* by Stuart Ross Taylor):

> The *Apollo II* landing on the moon took place on July 20, 1969, at 3:17:40 P.M., Eastern Standard Time, near the southern edge of Mare Tranquillitatis. [*medium-length sentence*] The site was named Tranquillity Base. [*short*] Astronauts Neil Armstrong and Edwin Aldrin collected 21.7 kilograms of samples in twenty minutes of hurried collecting toward the end of their two-hour sojourn (EVA, or extra vehicular activity) on the lunar surface. [*medium to long*] These samples were received in the quarantine facilities of the Lunar Receiving Laboratory in Houston on July 25. [*short*] Four weeks of intensive examination began. [*short*] A team of scientific workers (the Lunar Sample Preliminary Examination Team, or LSPET comprising eleven NASA scientists and fifteen other scientists from universities and government agencies) carried out preliminary geologic, geochemical, and biological examination of the samples, providing basic data for the Lunar Sample Analysis Planning Team (LSAPT). [*long*] Many of the first-order conclusions about the samples (such as their chemical uniqueness, their great age, and the absence of water, organic matter, and life) were established in this period. [*medium*]

Note the sequence of sentence lengths in Taylor's paragraph: medium/short/medium-long/short/short/long/medium.

VOICE ——————————— voice

Make your writing more direct by changing the verb from the passive voice to the active voice. (See _Emphasis._)

Verbs that take the direct object are in the active voice. In other words, when the verb is in the _active voice_, the subject of the sentence is doing the acting. When the verb is in the _passive voice_, the subject is being acted upon:

> **ACTIVE:** The referee blew the whistle. [The word _whistle_ is the direct object of _blew_, a verb in the _active voice._]

When the direct object becomes the subject, the verb changes to a form of the verb _to be_ plus a past participle and is said to be in the _passive voice_:

> **PASSIVE:** The whistle was blown by the referee. [The word _whistle_ in the previous example was a direct object, but now it is the subject. The verb _was blown_—form of **to** _be_ plus a past participle—is in the _passive voice._]

Notice how the following sentences are more direct in the active voice:

> **WEAK PASSIVE VOICE:** With the changing of seasons there comes a change in the type of clothing _to be worn._
> **DIRECT ACTIVE VOICE:** With the changing of seasons there comes a change in the type of clothing that _people wear._ [Even better: _With the changing of the seasons people change the type of clothing they wear._]

> **PASSIVE:** In the fall, cotton clothes _are stored_ away by families.
> **ACTIVE:** In the fall, _families store away_ their cotton clothes.

PASSIVE: This book *should be read by all of you* as soon as it *can be bought* in paperback.

ACTIVE: *You all should read* this book as soon as *you can buy* it in paperback.

Effective Uses of the Passive Voice

You may use the passive voice if the receiver of the action, or the action itself is more important than the doer of the action:

• The mayor of Regina *was bitten* by a horse today. [The *receiver* of the biting, the mayor of Regina, gets top billing in this sentence.]

• The restaurant fire *was started* by a dripping panful of hot grease. [The *action*, the fire, is of more interest than who or what started it.]

You may use the passive voice if the doer of the action is unknown:

• Some years ago a treasure-laden Spanish galleon *was recovered* not far from the coast of Florida. [The writer may not know who recovered it or simply may not find that detail worth mentioning.]

Except in cases when the passive voice is particularly needed, a careful writer will tend to avoid passive voice constructions because they can often lead to weak, roundabout, and wordy sentences.

wdy ———————————— WORDINESS

Express your ideas in fewer words.

Do not pad your sentences with unnecessary, repetitious phrasing. Avoid the unnecessary repetition of words and ideas:

WORDY: The novel, *Don Quixote*, by Cervantes, is a novel that satirizes the dying age of chivalry. [Why repeat the word novel? A simple revision cuts out *four* needless words.]
BETTER: The novel, *Don Quixote*, by Cervantes, satirizes the dying age of chivalry.

WORDY: *In my opinion, I personally believe* that our system of government is the best. [*In my opinion, personally,* and *I believe* are three ways of phrasing the same idea. Do not use them all at once.]
BETTER: I believe that our system of government is best.

WORDY: *In the modern world of today*, the human race is enjoying the fruits of a long technological revolution *that took place throughout the entire period of the machine age.*
BETTER: Today the human race is enjoying the fruits of a long technological revolution. [All that has been left out is repetition that adds nothing.]

WORDY: *We as humans* must address the problem of poverty.
BETTER: We must address the problem of poverty. [The phrase, *as humans*, is repetitive.]

(See **Repetition**.)

Where possible, use short, direct grammatical constructions:

INDIRECT: Satar made the salad, and *the cake was baked* by Sheena. [Use the active voice instead of the passive. See **Voice**.]
DIRECT: Satar made the salad, and Sheena baked the cake.

TOO LONG: I was responsible for overall maintenance, but *it was* Tran *who* did most of the repair jobs.

SHORTER: *I was* responsible for overall maintenance, but Tran did most of the repair jobs.

Some common wordy expressions to avoid:

Wordy	Concise
Along the line of	About
At that point in time	At that time (*or* At that point)
Crisis situation	Crisis
Due to the fact that (he objected)	Because (he objected)
Emergency situation	Emergency
For a long period of time	For a long time

Wordy	Concise
For the purpose of	For
In spite of the fact that (he left)	Despite (his leaving)
In the event that	If
The true facts	The facts

wp——— WORD PROCESSING

Thanks to commonly available word-processing systems, the physical task of revision has never been easier. Keep in mind, however, a few simple cautions regarding the preparation and submission of word-processed, paper copy ("hardcopy," as it is called) to your instructor:

- *"Saving" your work:* In the course of writing directly into your computer, avoid accidental losses by frequently saving your work—manually, at least once every paragraph; or by setting your "automatic save" function for intervals of no more than about fifteen to twenty minutes apart. Little is more depressing than losing hours and hours of work because of mechanical or electrical system failure. It is also extremely important to save your document even further—onto a diskette—in case your hard drive should fail!

- *Hardcopy:* If you can, always print out hardcopy at the end of each writing session. Many of you know by experience that you cannot trust electronic systems completely. Finally, when you are ready to hand in your completed hardcopy document, always keep at least one back-up hardcopy version of the document for your own files.

- *Formatting and Pagination:* Set your margins for between one and one and a half inches on all four sides, and always set your line-spacing to double-space, to provide ample room for your instructor's comments and revision symbols. Remember also to activate the page-numbering function of your system.

- *Fonts:* Most word-processing programs these days come with a great variety of fonts (styles of type). Avoid the temptation to use some weird or fancy font. Use something standard, like Courier or Prestige, or the "default" font (the one your system employs if you do not choose a different one). Unusual fonts call unnecessary attention to themselves and can be hard on your instructor's eyes. Do not use a font that is entirely in *italics* (slanted letters) either. Reserve italics for emphasis (see **Italics**). Finally, use a standard size font, preferably ten *cpi* (characters per inch) and ten to twelve *points* per character (*points* measure the size of each individual letter).

- *Spellcheckers, grammar checkers, etc.:* Automatic spellcheckers, dictionaries (thesauruses), and grammar checkers are sometimes helpful but totally mindless and often unreliable aids. Do not rely on them for the *major* work of correction and revision of your writing. Finally, *you* are solely responsible for all the problems eventually pointed out in your manuscript.

- ***Submission etiquette:*** Do not hand in a manuscript of fan-folded, unseparated sheets. Separate them and arrange them in proper numerical order. And, of course, be sure to remove the perforated edges of track-fed paper. Finally, be sure that the print is dark enough for your instructor to read with ease.

ww ——————— WRONG WORD

Keep a dictionary handy and, when you have any doubts about the exact meaning of a word, look up its definition before you use it.

Words Often Misused: A Glossary (See also *Diction*)

Accept/except. *Accept* means *to receive* or *to agree* to something: "I *accepted* his offer." *Except* used as a verb, can mean only *to exclude*: "He was *excepted* from the list of prize winners."

Affect/effect. As a verb, *affect* means *to influence*: "Her speech *affected* many people." To *effect* as a verb means *to bring about* or *to cause*: "It is hard to *effect* a change in society." As a noun, *affect* is a technical term for feeling. *Effect* as a noun means *result*: "The *effect* of the blow was to split the stone in half."

Aggravate. *Aggravate* means *to make worse*. It is not a synonym for *irritate* or *annoy*. Do not write: "His snide remarks *aggravated* me." Write: "His snide remarks irritated me." Further insults would, of course, *aggravate* your irritation.

Allusion/illusion. An *allusion* is an indirect reference; an *illusion* is a false or deceptive notion.

Alot/a lot. *Alot* is simply a misspelling of *a lot*. In formal writing, however, it is usually better to use *many, much,* or *very much* instead of *a lot*.

Alright. In formal English, this is an unacceptable spelling of *all right*.

Among/between. Ordinarily, *between* is used when only two items are spoken of: "I divided the food *between* the cat and the dog." *Among* relates to more than two items: "The prize money was divided *among* the three winners."

Amount/number. When things or people can be counted individually, use *number*: "I saw a large *number* of students in the hall." When you are referring to a quantity of something that is not thought of as individual, countable units, use *amount*: "A large *amount* of gold was discovered in the mountain."

And/or. Use this compound sparingly and only in a highly technical or legalistic context.

Anyways/anywheres. Use the standard forms *anyway* and *anywhere*.

Around. Do not use the colloquial *around* in expressions like "He left *around* ten o'clock." "I can recite *around* fifteen poems." Use *about*: "He left *about* ten o'clock." "I can recite *about* fifteen poems."

As. *As*, in the sense of *because*, is often not as clear as *because*, *for*, or *since*. "I would like to leave *because* [not *as*] I'm tired." (See **Like**.)

At. (See **Where at**.)

Awhile/a while. After a preposition, spell as two words: "I slept for *a while*." Otherwise spell as one word: "I slept *awhile*."

Bad/badly. After the verbs *feel, look, taste, smell, sound*, use the adjective *bad*, not the adverb *badly* (See **Adjectives**, 1.)

Because. (See **Reason is because**.)

Because of the fact that. The phrase *because of the fact that* is unnecessarily wordy. Simply use *because*.

Being as/being that. *Because* or *since* are preferred in standard English.

Beside/besides. *Beside* means *at the side of*; *besides* means *in addition to*. "*Besides* chicken, we ate roast beef and bananas as we sat *beside* the stream."

Bust/busted. These are slang forms of the verb *burst*. Use *burst* in present and past tenses. *Bursted* is nonstandard.

Capital/capitol. Use the *-al* version when you mean a *capital city* of a province or country (like Halifax, Nova Scotia), *capital punishment* (the death penalty), or *capital* in the sense of assets. Use the *-ol* version when you mean a provincial *capitol*—the building in which a provincial legislature conducts its business—or the *Capitol* in Washington, D.C., where the the U.S. Congress meets.

Centres around/centre on. In formal English use *centres on*: "The global economy still *centres on* oil production." Remember that the American spelling of this word is *center*.

Choose/Chose. A spelling mixup. *Choose* is the present tense of the verb to *choose*; *chose* is the past tense. (See also **Loose/lose**.)

Compare to/compare with. *To compare to* means to find resemblances in things that are otherwise quite different: "He *compared* the coffee *to* mud." *To compare with* means to find similarities and differences between two things that are of the same sort: "He *compared* the female students *with* the male students and found that the females were brighter."

Could of. This term is illiterate for *could have*, which in speech is often contracted to *could've* and misspelled *could of* [As a general rule, avoid contractions in formal writing.]

Data. This word is a Latin plural (singular, *datum*) and is often used in English with plural verbs and pronouns: "*These* data *are* out of date." Many people accept its use in the singular: "*This* data *is* no longer useful." (See **Phenomena**; **Strata**.)

Don't. *Don't* is a contraction of *do not* and should not be confused with *does not* or *doesn't*. Nonstandard: "He *don't* mind insults." Standard: "He *doesn't* [or *does not*] mind insults."

Bear in mind that contractions are acceptable in speech but not in formal writing.

Due to. Use *due to* only to connect a noun construction with another noun construction: "*Rickets* [noun] is *due to* a vitamin D *deficiency* [noun]." Do not use it to connect nouns with main clauses: Wrong: "Due to an *accident* [noun] *the traffic was backed up for miles* [main clause]." (If you are uncertain, use *because of* or *caused by*, whichever fits.)

Due to the fact that. Avoid being wordy. Use *because*.

Effect. (See **Affect/effect**.)

Enthuse. In formal English, it is better to use *to be enthusiastic*.

Equally as good. Drop the *as* and write *equally good*, or use *just as good*.

Etc. This is short for the Latin *et cetera*, meaning *and so on* or *and so forth*. Avoid *etc*.: It is often a substitute for precise and detailed thinking. (See **Abbreviations**.)

Except. (See **Accept/except**.)

Farther/further. *Farther* is often preferred to express extent in space, whereas *further* is preferred to express extent in time or degree: "We walked *farther* into the woods." "He went *further* in condemning him than anyone expected."

Favourite. Because *favourite* is already a superlative, meaning "most liked, most favoured," to combine it with another superlative, "*most* favourite," is redundant. (See **Unique**.)

Fewer/less. When referring to separate items that can be counted, use *fewer*: "You make *fewer* mistakes now than when you started." *Less* refers to the degree or amount of something we consider as a whole and not as a series of individual items: "I have *less* money now than when I started."

Flaunt/flout. To *flaunt* is to show off, as in the TV commercial of some years back: "If you've got it, *flaunt* it." To *flout* is to show contempt for: "He *flouted* all the rules and did things his own way."

Hadn't ought. *Hadn't ought* is nonstandard for *should not*. Instead of writing, "I *hadn't ought* to have gone," write, "I *should not* have gone."

Healthful/healthy. Whatever *gives* health is *healthful* ("a *healthful* climate"), and whatever *has* health is *healthy* ("a *healthy* person").

Illusion. (See **Allusion/illusion**.)

In regards to. Use *in regard to*.

Irregardless. The proper form is *regardless*.

It's. A contraction of *it is* and a common misspelling of the possessive pronoun *its*: "They examined *its* [not *it's*] contents." Use *it's*, and other contractions, only in *informal* written English and in recording actual *speech*.

Kind of/sort of. *Kind of* and *sort of* are informal expressions. In formal written English, use *somewhat, rather, a little*: "She was *somewhat* [not *kind of*] annoyed."

Lay/lie. When you mean *to put*, use *lay*. The forms of *to lay* are "I *lay* the book down" (present), "I *laid* the book down" (past), and "I *have laid* the book down" (present perfect). When you mean *to recline*, use *lie*. The forms of *to lie* are "I *lie* in my bed" (present), "I *lay* in my bed" (past), and "I *have lain* in my bed" (present perfect).

Layed. Incorrect spelling of *laid*. (See **Lay/lie**.)

Lead/led. A spelling mixup: The past tense of *to lead* is *led*, not *lead*.

Less. (See **Fewer/less**.)

Like/as/as if. *Like* is a preposition and is properly used in a phrase such as the following: "He looks *like* my father." It is improperly used when followed by a clause.

MISUSE: "It looks *like* my father enjoys your company."

NOTE: A clause is a group of words containing a subject and a verb. In the example just given, *father* is the subject and *enjoys* is the verb of the clause "my father enjoys your company."

> **REVISION:** Change *like* to *as if*: "It looks *as if* my father enjoys your company." In the sentence "I behaved *like* I was told to," change *like* to *as*, "I behaved *as* I was told to."

Loose/lose. A spelling mixup: *Loose* (pronounced *loos*) means "slack," as in "a loose knot." *Lose* (pronounced *looz*) is the verb "to lose," as in "to lose a fortune."

May of/might of. The terms *may of* and *might of* are illiterate for *may have, might have*. (See **Could of.**)

Media. *Media* is the plural form of *medium*; it takes a plural verb: "Some advertising *media* are morally harmful, and the *medium* that sins the most in this respect is television." A singular verb with *media* is nonstandard. (See **Data; Phenomena; Strata.**)

Mighty. Use a standard word like *very*: "I was *very* [not *mighty*] tired."

Most. Use *almost*: "I saw them *almost* [not *most*] every day."

Must of. This term is illiterate for *must have*. (See **Could of.**)

Off of. Drop the *of*.

Phenomena. In formal English, *phenomena* is the plural, *phenomenon* the singular.

Principal/principle. *Principal* can be used as an adjective (*chief, main, highest-ranking*: She has the *principal* role in the play) or noun (referring to a *leader*, as of a high school; or referring to *capital*, in financial usage). It has nothing to do with the noun *principle*, meaning a basic truth or belief (the *principles* of democracy), or a scientific rule or law (the *principles* of biomechanics).

Quite. Do not overuse *quite* to mean *very*, as in *quite* good, *quite* hard.

Real/really. Keep expressions like *real good* and *really exciting* out of your written English. Use *very good*.

Reason is because. In informal usage you may hear: "The *reason* I told you *is because* I can trust you." *Because* is redundant. See also the example under **Mixed Construction**. For formal writing, revise as follows. *Method 1:* The reason I told you is *that* I can trust you. [*Because* changed to *that*.] *Method 2:* I told you because I can trust you. [The sentence has been recast.]

Set/Sit. Do not use *set* (to place something somewhere: "I *set* my suitcase down.") when you mean *sit* or *sat* ("She was glad to *sit* down."). Nonstandard: "Johnny stormed in and *set* down at the bar." Standard: "Johnny stormed in and *sat* down at the bar."

Should of. The term *should of* is illiterate for *should have*. (See **Could of**.)

So. (1) Do not overuse *so* as a conjunction joining main clauses. (See **Subordination**). (2) Do not use *so* where you could use *so that*. Change "I came to visit you *so* we could have a chat" to "I came to visit you *so that* we could have a chat." (3) Do not overuse *so* as an intensifier: "I was *so* disappointed." "She is *so* nice, isn't she?" Try substituting *very* or *extremely*.

Sort of. (See **Kind of**.)

Strata. Use *strata* only as a plural, not as a singular, noun. The singular is *stratum*. Nonstandard: He came from an extremely disadvantaged *strata* of society. Standard: He came from an extremely disadvantaged *stratum* of society.

Sure. Use *certainly* or *surely* "I *certainly* [not *sure*] was tired."

That/which. *Which*, rather than *that*, should be used with nonrestrictive clauses, in other words, with clauses that do not change the basic meaning of the sentence.

Their/there/they're. Do not confuse the possessive pronoun *their* (*my, your, their*) with the *there* that points to a particular place (She lives *there*), or with the idiomatic expression *there is*, *there are* (*There are* many varieties of English), or with *they're*, a contraction of *they are*.

Then/than. *Then* is sometimes a misspelling of *than*. Than is used in comparisons: "They would rather die *than* surrender." *Then* means *consequently* or *as a result*, or it refers to time and means *next* or *at that time*: "If the sun is a dying star, *then* the Earth is doomed to extinction." "He came, he saw, and *then* he turned around and left."

To/too/two. *To* is a preposition. See **Variety in Sentence Patterns** ("Using a Prepositional Phrase"). *Too* means *also*. Do not confuse the *two* (the number 2).

Try and. *Try and* is an informal version of *try to*: "I am going to *try and* help my neighbour." In formal English, write: "I am going to *try to* help my neighbour."

Unique. Because *unique*, meaning "unlike any other," describes the quality of being beyond comparison, do not combine it with adverbs of comparison or degree like "more unique," "most unique," and "very or rather unique." It makes no sense to write "Jorge's style is *more unique* than Carol's" since you cannot compare something which is entirely unlike anything else. (See also entry for *Favourite*.)

Where at. In a sentence like "I know *where* he is *at*," at is unnecessary and should be dropped: "I know *where* he is."

Which/that. (See **That/which**.)

Which, who. Use *who* (or that, but never use *which* to refer to persons. "Here is the man *who* [not *which*] is responsible."

While. *While* is mainly a conjunction of time: "I ran *while* I still had time." Do not overwork it to mean *and, but,* or *whereas*: "I loved roses, *but* [not *while*] she preferred daisies."

Whose, who's. A spelling mixup. See **Case**, 7.

Would of. The term *would of* is illiterate for *would have*. (See **Could of**.)

APPENDIX I

THE WRITING PROCESS

The greatest danger in writing is the assumption that you know what to say and how to say it. The old adage in Composition and Rhetoric classes is that there is no such thing as good writing; there is only good rewriting. You may know what you are attempting to communicate, but you cannot assume that your reader will be able to follow your thinking.

When you are taking a vacation, you do not simply jump into your car and go; instead, you go through a process. This process involves planning your route, organizing your itinerary, setting out, and revising based upon events that you encounter. The same is true with your writing. You need to use an effective process in order to write effectively. While this handbook focuses on the revision side of writing, you should think about the whole process of composition.

Successful writing is powerful communication. This is a simple way to remember the writing process. Communication is POWeR. Remember the word POWeR. It means Plan Organize Write and Revise. POWeR is a four-step process to effective writing.

Step 1: Plan

There are two parts to planning. These are deciding what you want to say, and generating material.

Deciding what you want to say is a function of the scope of your writing. If, for example, you are asked to write a 500 word report for the manager of your structural engineering company, a topic such as "causes for structural failure" is far too large. There are simply too many things that you could discuss to make any meaningful or powerful statement. Limiting the scope to something like "structural failure of bridges due to harmonic resonance" may be more manageable within the 500 word scope; even this may be too large. Use the length guidelines you are given to help you narrow the scope of your paper. Make a decision about what you want to discuss and write it down. This will help you to focus your thinking for the balance of the planning stage.

The planning stage continues on to what you are going to say. Use techniques such as brainstorming, freewriting, or research to identify your ideas and areas that will need research. There are six questions that you want to answer. These are who, what, why, when, where and how. Keep in mind that planning is an iterative process; you should always back up and go through the process again, particularly if you find yourself stuck.

When brainstorming, keep your pen in hand and let your mind wander freely around your topic. Jot down anything that comes to mind, no matter how irrelevant it may seem. You can filter your ideas at the next stage. With brainstorming, you are not concerned with the expression of ideas; rather, you are simply concerned with getting the ideas down on paper. You can round them out later through focused freewriting or research.

Freewriting, like brainstorming, has you generate ideas. But this time, instead of letting your mind wander freely, you focus your thinking around a specific idea and expand upon it. Focused freewriting is generally used to expand upon the ideas generated through brainstorming.

Research is used to expand and validate the ideas developed through brainstorming and freewriting. When researching, either through library books and journals, through on-line investigations, or through personal contacts, remember to keep track of your information for documentation purposes (see **Documentation**).

2. Organize, or Outline

Organizing entails putting your ideas and research into an order that flows logically from your topic to your conclusion. Here you will make a series of decisions: what order do I want?

what do I need to support this point? what is the relationship between ideas? Often, you will find that in the process of organizing and outlining your writing, there are aspects you may have missed in content generation. This is the time to go back and fill in the gaps. Remember that writing is iterative.

The best writing flows out of the best outlines. In this stage of the writing process, you are really thinking through your whole essay. The more detail that you can put into your outline, the easier the writing of your first draft will be. Often, students and professionals try to short-cut this step. This is a mistake. The more thought that you put into your planning and organizing, the easier the rest of the writing process will be.

In organizing an outline, there are a few questions to ask yourself.

1. What is the overall point of my writing?
2. How do individual paragraphs lead to this point?
3. What point do I want to make in this particular paragraph?
4. What points do I need to make to complete the overall point of the paragraph?
5. How do my ideas flow into the paragraph?
6. How do my paragraphs hold together?
7. Is anything missing?

If your answer to number 7 is yes, return to the planning stage.

3. Write

If your outline is exhaustive, the act of writing should be fairly spontaneous. If you find yourself wondering what you will say next, return to your planning and organizing stages.

When you actually begin to write from your outline, do not worry about things like grammar and usage. There will be time for that in the revision stage. The purpose of the writing stage is to get your ideas down on paper, in complete sentences and paragraphs. There is an old rule of thumb to remember: it is easy to change something that exists—but until it exists, you can't change it. Revision, the purpose of this handbook, is the next stage.

If you find that your writing bogs down—that you don't know what to say next—back up in your process. Try brainstorming and focused freewriting again; make a secondary outline for your next paragraph. There is nothing wrong with thinking things through a second time. There is a problem with going ahead blindly and thoughtlessly.

4. Revise

This is the point of this handbook. Don't assume that your writing is perfect. Nobody writes perfectly. Everybody makes mistakes. The trick to good writing is knowing how to identify and correct your personal errors.

The Common Error Chart included with this book is your best starting point for grammatical inconsistencies. Keep track of the errors which your professors note on your papers. This will help you to zero in on the parts of sentences to which you should pay special attention. But don't trust your common error chart alone.

Compare your final writing to your outline and your brainstorming. Did you include everything that you intended to include? Did you miss anything? As you read through your paper, do you see a logical flow from its topic or thesis, through its support, to its conclusion? Should anything be added or deleted? Ultimately, the question which you need to ask yourself is "Will my reader agree with my conclusion?" If your answer to this question is yes, and if you are grammatically correct, you should do well on the paper. If you can anticipate any reason for your reader to disagree with your conclusion, you should go back to the writing process and build your response to this disagreement into your paper.

5. The Last Step

Your last step is preparing the paper for presentation and handing it in to your professor or your boss for evaluation. If you have used a consistent process for your writing; if you have anticipated and responded to the needs and expectations of your audience; if you have revised for consistency, you should do well. You have achieved POWeR through written communication.

INDEX*

*Capitalized entries are section titles. Italicized entries are from "Words Often Misused: A Glossary" under the **Wrong Word** section. Italicized page numbers are for main entries.

INDEX